T0277459

Cambridge Elements

Elements in Beckett Studies
edited by
Dirk Van Hulle
University of Oxford
Mark Nixon
University of Reading

BECKETT'S INTERMEDIAL ECOSYSTEMS

Closed Space Environments across the Stage, Prose and Media Works

Anna McMullan
University of Reading

CAMBRIDGE
UNIVERSITY PRESS

CAMBRIDGE
UNIVERSITY PRESS

University Printing House, Cambridge CB2 8BS, United Kingdom

One Liberty Plaza, 20th Floor, New York, NY 10006, USA

477 Williamstown Road, Port Melbourne, VIC 3207, Australia

314–321, 3rd Floor, Plot 3, Splendor Forum, Jasola District Centre,
New Delhi – 110025, India

79 Anson Road, #06–04/06, Singapore 079906

Cambridge University Press is part of the University of Cambridge.

It furthers the University's mission by disseminating knowledge in the pursuit of
education, learning, and research at the highest international levels of excellence.

www.cambridge.org
Information on this title: www.cambridge.org/9781108959056
DOI: 10.1017/9781108938990

© Anna McMullan 2021

First published 2021

A catalogue record for this publication is available from the British Library.

ISBN 978-1-108-95905-6 Paperback
ISSN 2632-0746 (online)
ISSN 2632-0738 (print)

Beckett's Intermedial Ecosystems

Closed Space Environments across the Stage, Prose and Media Works

Elements in Beckett Studies

DOI: 10.1017/9781108938990
First published online: January 2021

Anna McMullan
University of Reading

Author for correspondence: Anna McMullan, a.e.mcmullan@reading.ac.uk

Abstract: This Element draws on the concept of ecosystems to investigate selected Beckett works across different media which present worlds where the human does not occupy a privileged place in the order of creation: rather Beckett's human figures are trapped in a regulated system in which they have little agency. Readers, listeners or viewers are complicit in the operation of techniques of observation inherent to the system, but are also reminded of the vulnerability of those subjected to it. Beckett's work offers new paradigms and practices which reposition the human in relation to space, time and species.

Keywords: Beckett, ecology, intermediality, anthropocene, climate crisis

ISBNs: 9781108959056 (PB), 9781108938990 (OC)
ISSNs: 2632-0746 (online), 2632-0738 (print)

Contents

1 Introduction

Beckett's textual and audiovisual imaginings of ruined worlds on the edge of extinction are remarkably prescient for a twenty-first century confronting a global climate emergency, where many species have already become extinct, and, according to David Wallace-Wells, we are facing the prospect of 'the liveable planet darkening as it approaches a human dusk' (2019, 16). Beckett's post–World War II work was written in the shadow of Hiroshima and Nagasaki, the Cold War and the fear of global nuclear destruction, but the blasted earth of *Happy Days*, the external devastation outside the refuge of *Endgame* or the desiccated climate and bodies of *Imagination Dead Imagine* are also extraordinarily redolent of our damaged planet given the rapidly increasing effects of human intervention upon the earth's environment. Beckett's texts combine a relentless interrogation of the will to power of the human species with a poetic resonance that articulates the experience of loss, vulnerability and dispossession, and his work remains vitally relevant as we confront the contemporary ecological crisis.

Greg Garrard defines the burgeoning multidisciplinary field of ecologically concerned criticism, or ecocriticism, as 'the study of the relationship of the human and the non-human throughout human cultural history and entailing critical analysis of the term "human" itself' (2012a, 5).[1] According to Carl Lavery and Clare Finburgh, much contemporary ecocriticism 'consciously sets out to place the so-called exceptionalism of the human subject in crisis' (2015, 12). Without homogenising a diverse set of discourses and practices, we might say that ecocriticism includes the repositioning of humans, the *anthropos*, not as masters of the earth's inhabitants and resources, but as cohabitants of the planet with other species. However, (some) humans have dominated and exploited other creatures and resources to such an extent, especially since the technological advances of the industrial age, that they have caused major impact upon and indeed damage to the earth's environment. This impact is reflected in debates about whether we are now entering, or are in, a new age – that of the Anthropocene, rather than the Holocene age which began about 11,700 years ago at the end of the last ice age. The term was introduced initially by Eugene Stoermer and then Paul Crutzen,[2] and, although the International Union of Geological Sciences has not yet formally declared the Anthropocene as a geological time unit (Zalasiewicz et al., 2017),[3] the concept has been taken up in critical debates in both the sciences and the humanities.

---

[1] The foundational text of ecocriticism is usually identified as Rachel Carson's *Silent Spring* published in 1962, which investigated the environmental impact of the indiscriminate use of pesticides in the United States.

[2] See Crutzen (2002).

[3] The Working Group on the Anthropocene, set up in 2009, presented its interim report to the International Union of Geological Sciences in August 2016 (see Zalasiewicz et al., 2017).

Scholars such as Zoe Todd (Davis and Todd, 2017) and Isabelle Stengers (2014) warn that terms such as 'Anthropocene' or 'anthropocentrism' are potentially problematic as they may erase the many differences and inequalities amongst human individuals and populations, reinforce the focus on humans rather than on other inhabitants of the earth, and neglect the fact that humans are also animals. Nevertheless, given these important provisos, Timothy Morton (2014) suggests that the term helps us to shift scale, placing human history or even prehistory within a larger perspective in space (the planet or universe) and time (a temporality before and indeed beyond the human species).[4] It has also become a useful critical tool for the analysis of the theological, scientific, philosophical, perceptual and representational systems which underpin anthropocentrism (David and Turpin, 2015), and, in particular, the rise of hierarchical systems of knowledge and classification rooted in European scientific, rational and colonial discourses and practices, which reasserted certain humans as masters of the rest of creation.[5]

Such a critique of humans as 'lords and possessors of nature', as Descartes puts it in *A Discourse on the Method of Correctly Conducting One's Reason and Seeking Truth in the Sciences* (Descartes, [1637] 2006, 51), chimes with Beckett's frequent comments on human indifference towards or drive to control others. For example, his 1957 radio play *All That Fall* conjures a remarkably diverse world of flora and fauna through sound effects and the reflections of the ageing and infirm Maddy Rooney as she walks to the station to meet her blind husband, Dan, on his birthday. Although the play is very specifically located in time (post-independence Ireland) and milieu (a small middle-class Protestant community in the environs of Dublin), much wider spatio-temporal frames are evoked that place the human in relation to the non-human or the more than human.[6] Maddy encounters layers of human technology and intervention during her journey which enact a history of the Anthropocene from the invention of the horse-driven cart, to the bicycle, the motor car and, finally, the monstrous train associated with the Industrial Revolution. The text stresses the '*exaggerated station sounds*' that should herald the arrival of the train with 'great hissing of steam and clashing of couplings' (Beckett, 1986, 187). Each of these incrementally

---

[4] See also Morton's concept of 'hyperobjects', such as global warming, which are ungraspable by humans because of their massive scale in space and time (Morton, 2013).

[5] Terms such as 'technocene' or 'capitalocene' have been proposed to account for the role of technology and capitalism in enabling some sectors of the human species to become dominant through increasing exploitation not only of the Earth's resources, but also of 'the exchange networks, the financial networks, extraction practices, wealth creations, and (mal)distributions in relation to both people and other critters' (Haraway, 2015, 259).

[6] The phrase 'more-than-human', sometimes though not always hyphenated, was coined by David Abram in *The Spell of the Sensuous: Perception and Language in a More-than-Human World* (1996) and is now frequently used in ecological discourses to refer to the non-human living world.

more powerful machines proves increasingly disastrous for the more than human species, from the hinny that Christy wallops, to the hen run over by Mr Slocum's car, and also for humans, since the reason for the delay of the twelve-thirty train is that a child was killed by falling under its wheels (the reason for the child's fall is never confirmed). Moreover, the other humans Maddy meets on her journey are mostly unsympathetic and indeed violent. Although Christy with his cart and Mr Tyler on his bicycle are friendly enough, Mr Slocum regrets offering Maddy a lift in his motor car, and Miss Fitt has to be shamed into lending Maddy a helping arm in order to ascend the steep path leading to the station: 'Your arm! Any arm! A helping hand! For five seconds! Christ what a planet! … Pismires do it for one another. [*Pause*] I have seen slugs do it' (Beckett, 1986, 183). In addition to the attempts of everyone else on the platform to ignore or get away from Maddy, there are acts of human-on-human violence: in a sound cue that might be overlooked (see Frost, 1997, 217–18), Mr Barrell delivers a '*backhanded blow in the stomach*' to young Tommy the station porter after several earlier threats (Beckett, 1986, 184), and, on their journey from the station, Maddy and Dan hear the cries of Mrs Tully, whose husband 'is in constant pain and beats her unmercifully' (193). In general, although Maddy herself is sympathetically attuned to the living world around her, humans come across as a species indifferent or destructive towards other creatures, and are unlikely to come to the aid of their fellow beings unless compelled to. In Beckett's later work, such a diverse environment has dwindled to an enclosed, regulated space only barely able to sustain life, where human bodies are the only inhabitants. I refer to these closed worlds as ecosystems.

Features of ecosystems, which may be tiny (a rockpool) or immense (the planet), include the interrelated networks that define the conditions of life in the system: '*An ecosystem is the interacting system made up of all the living and non-living objects in a specified volume of space*' (Weathers, Strayer and Likens, 2013, 3; italics in original). However, ecosystems are also constructs whose boundaries are defined by the scientific observer:

> The study of an ecosystem requires defining boundaries. Thus, ecosystems are places defined by investigators [. . .] The ultimate goal of ecosystem research is not to reduce or isolate specific components but rather to understand the system that results from the interactions of the components as a whole. (Weathers, Strayer and Likens, 2013, 181)[7]

---

[7] The acknowledgement of ecosystems as units of analysis defined by the scientist goes back to the first use of the term 'ecosystem' by ecologist Arthur Tansley in 1935: 'The whole method of science [. . .] is to isolate systems mentally for the purposes of study [. . .] The isolation is partly artificial, but is the only possible way in which we can proceed' (Tansley, 1935, 299–300).

I argue that this concept of a system whose boundaries are externally determined in order to create a microcosm with human specimens that can be inspected is relevant to much of Beckett's work across different media. His microcosms, however, are not slices of the living world, but models of alternative worlds in which the *anthropos* is placed under observation. It is therefore not only the conditions of the ecosystem that are of interest, but also how the ecosystem is defined, created and observed.[8]

Beckett's work is being increasingly explored from an ecocritical perspective which focuses on the interrelationship between humans, other creatures and the environment in his writing. In her introduction to a special issue of *Samuel Beckett Today / Aujourd'hui* on Beckett and the non-human, Amanda Dennis argues that 'attending to the nonhuman enhances our understanding of the limits and responsibilities of the human vis-à-vis a planet in crisis' (Dennis, 2020, 152). Mary Bryden refers to Beckett's 'species consciousness' (2013, 3),[9] and she and other scholars have examined how Beckett often 'animalises' his human creatures, emphasising their material, embodied existence, refocusing attention from the human towards a range of more than human species (horses, rats or fleas, for example) that cohabit the narrative worlds of his texts, or, in the later work, portraying humans as objects of observation within their often restrictive habitats.[10] Scholars have also examined the elements that constitute the biospheres in which Beckett's creatures exist, including the atmosphere (Connor, 2003) and the weather (Davies, 2006). Paul Davies draws attention to the absence of the natural environment in the closed mindscapes or 'womb-tombs' of the later work – what he calls 'the condition of human alienation from the biosphere' (2006, 74). Greg Garrard (2012a) and Joe Kelleher (2015) acknowledge the overt references to a historically devastated environment in *Endgame* and *Happy Days* respectively.

Scholars approaching Beckett's work from an ecological perspective agree that such readings need to go beyond the literal level of representation or

---

[8] Important studies of the operation of systems in Beckett's work include, for example, Garin Dowd's *Abstract Machines: Samuel Beckett and Philosophy after Deleuze and Guattari* (2007), Enoch Brater's article on Andy Warhol and Samuel Beckett, which focuses on the operation of seriality in Beckett's work (1974), and Harry White's discussion of musical serialism (1998). I use the concept of systems in a more ecological sense, though at times I draw on complementary scholarship on Beckett and confinement (Little, 2020), medium-specific systems (Pattie, 2018) and technology (Kiryushina, Adar and Nixon, 2021).

[9] *How It Is* makes several references to 'loss of species' (Beckett, 1964, 29) or having 'clung on to the species' (52).

[10] See Weller (2008) and (2013). Joseph Anderton's *Beckett's Creatures: Art of Failure after the Holocaust* (2016) challenges anthropocentric uses of the term 'human' in his discussion of 'creaturely life' in Beckett's work, though the focus of the book is primarily on how 'the Second World War and the Holocaust transformed, or rather revealed, the idea of the human as people had witnessed its creaturely potential' (20).

content. Beckett was evidently not an eco-activist concerned with saving the planet – indeed, salvation of any kind is always a myth in Beckett's work – but his texts might be aligned with what Timothy Morton has called the ecological way of thinking (Morton, 2010), which decentres the place of the human and emphasises rather the interconnectedness of all elements in the planet's ecosystem. Carl Lavery has argued that Beckett's theatre performs such a repositioning of the human. Lavery offers a detailed assessment of Beckett's approach to the medium of the theatre as an enclosed space cut off from the 'chaos of everyday life', not to 'eject or deny the world in an act of spurious aesthetic autonomy, but to find another way of engaging with it' (2018a, 17). This other way is attentive to the expanded experience of both time and species that Beckett's work offers: 'In Beckett's hands, theatre is no longer a space where the essence of the human appears; on the contrary, it is a site where the human dis-appears, subjected, as it is, to a series of "more than human" flows and processes that challenge its much-vaunted exceptionalism and apparent omniscience' (11).

This monograph takes its point of departure from Lavery's interest in Beckett's creation of worlds that recalibrate our experience of time and space in relation to the human.[11] I am interested in Beckett's use of each medium in shaping the conditions of production, communication and reception of these worlds, whether reading or hearing / watching. I focus on those works that evoke an (apparently) hermetic environment, a motif that is usually analysed in relation to what scholars have termed Beckett's 'closed space' texts, referring to a series of prose texts from the 1960s, including *All Strange Away*, *Imagination morte imaginez* / *Imagination Dead Imagine*, the 'Faux départs' fragments, 'Bing' / 'Ping', *Fizzle* VIII 'Endroit clos' / 'Closed Space' and *Le Dépeupleur* / *The Lost Ones* (written in various stages from the mid-to-late 1960s).[12] However, this Element explores Beckett's closed spaces from a transmedial and intermedial perspective,[13] tracing the motif back to an unpublished

---

[11] See also Steven Connor's discussion of Beckett's work as 'short of world' in relation to Heidegger's concept of worlding in Connor (2006, n.p.). Connor argues that 'Beckett has a strong sense of what Heidegger might call "worlding", the creation of worlds. But his characters and narrators live, not within "the world" or worlds as such, but within *Umwelts* that they constitute from themselves, or are constituted from themselves, not voluntarily, but unavoidably.'

[12] See Pilling (2006, 166–85) for dates of composition of these texts. Scholars who have used the term 'closed space' to group these texts include Ruby Cohn (2001, 285) and Stan Gontarski (2017, 62–74). I generally use the English titles of Beckett's works except when the era of composition or the French text is specifically mentioned. In such cases as here, the title is given in French where the work was originally composed in French, followed by the English translation.

[13] The prefix 'trans' is taken here to refer to the recurrence of the trope or recreation of closed worlds across the different media in which Beckett worked, whereas the term 'intermedial' is used primarily as Christopher Balme defines it: 'the attempt to realise in one medium the

dramatic fragment from the early 1950s, 'Espace souterrain', and investigates Beckett's interest in mime during the 1950s and 1960s as an imaginative technique for envisioning or modelling the relationship between human figures and a highly regulated environment.[14] I then analyse a selection of the closed space prose texts of the 1960s, which have often been described as 'wombtomb' or skull spaces. James Little's monograph *Samuel Beckett in Confinement: The Politics of Closed Space* (2020) also takes a cross-disciplinary and interdisciplinary approach to Beckett's closed space texts, emphasising the deeply political dimensions of Beckett's closed space aesthetic and its embodied and institutional resonances. However, the focus of this Element is the argument that Beckett's closed space texts combine qualities of confined interior space with the sense of a cosmological or ecological system: we might think of these texts as evoking damaged, exhausted or entropic habitations, cosmologies or biospheres, where the systems of heat and light have become polarised and extreme: *All Strange Away*'s '[s]ame system light and heat with sweat more or less, cringing away from walls, burning soles, now one, now the other' (Beckett, 1995, 171); the 'passage from heat and light to black and cold' (183) of *Imagination Dead Imagine*, or the oscillation of the temperature between hot and cold in *The Lost Ones*.

I argue that the confined space systems of these works continue to metamorphose across other texts and media throughout the next years and indeed right up to the strict patterns of movement in *Quad* (a televisual reworking of the abandoned 'J. M. Mime' from 1963) and the 1983 stage play *What Where*, subsequently revised for television. As part of their trajectory, the qualities of these closed spaces also shift in emphasis, from the sociopolitical resonances of some of the early dramatic fragments and mimes to the exhausted biospheres of *Imagination Dead Imagine* and *The Lost Ones*, to the observation chamber of *All Strange Away* and some of the television plays. Such a perspective draws attention to the role of the medium itself in the construction and reader or spectator perception of those environments, as well as suggesting ways in which they begin to be crafted intermedially. In other words, Beckett translates his experience of working in one medium into his exploration of the boundaries of another and how it creates a world.[15]

---

aesthetic conventions and habits of seeing and hearing in another medium' (2004, 7). See, for example, Chapple and Kattenbelt (2006), Pethö (2011) and *Samuel Beckett Today / Aujourd'hui* 32.1 on Beckett and Intermediality (McTighe, Morin and Nixon, 2020).

[14] University of Reading Beckett Collection, MS 2931 and MS 2932.

[15] Although this Element occasionally refers to Beckett's radio plays, it does not include a specific section on radio. This is partly because I have written in detail on *All That Fall* from an ecological point of view elsewhere (forthcoming, 2021), for reasons of space, and also because Beckett's

These texts intensify the pervasive rejection or parody in Beckett's work of the concept of a sovereign, human, rational subject or agent who exercises control over the external environment through technology or *technè* (a will to make or create). Yet these subjected bodies have been brought into being through the agency of their author, and indeed, in the case of Beckett's drama for stage and audiovisual media, by their creative and technical teams. Beckett's closed space texts both model worlds in which the human is reduced to an exhausted species in a shrunken environment, and reflect on the modes of authority which produce them, drawing attention to their own mechanisms of generation and control. The concept of ecosystem therefore relates not only to the fictional environment invoked by narrative or audiovisual means, but also to the material and techno-logical affordances and constraints of the medium itself. Frequently, the works turn the drive to observe and control creation, which would be attributed to divine or supernatural beings in non-secular cultures, against humans themselves. Indeed, the framework of a world whose creation and laws may be regulated by an external power, whether divine or infernal, is posited in several works, and often linked back to Dante's cosmology, as in *How It Is*, opening up 'vast tracts of time' beyond that of human history (Beckett, 1964, 7). However, the nature of who or what regulates the environment that Beckett's creatures inhabit most often remains unclear or beyond cognition, though ultimately the works reflect on their own increasingly depleted conditions of creation or imagining. How these works then position their readers or spectators engages them in confronting ways of seeing and responding to both human and more than human creatures that question the histories, knowledges and technologies of anthropocentric agency.

The second section draws on the concept of the stage as the model of an ecosystem. Citing the work of Bonnie Marranca in *Ecologies of Theatre*, Clare Finburgh and Carl Lavery argue that 'theatrical texts or productions can be like ecosystems – collectives of interrelating and interdependent scenic elements on stage' (2015, 15). When directing *Endgame* for the Schiller Theater in 1967, Beckett famously commented to Michael Haerdter: 'There for me lies the value of the theatre. One turns out a small world with its own laws, conducts the action as if upon a chessboard' (McMillan and Fehsenfeld, 1988, 231). Chess here operates as a metaphor for a self-contained fictional microcosm. This section relates the

---

experimentation in the radio medium was concentrated into a relatively short time frame: 1956 to the early 1960s. Although the radio plays parallel the increasing concern with the perceptual conditions and technical affordances of the medium itself characteristic of Beckett's work in other media, I wanted to focus on Beckett's shift into the visual media of film and television in the mid-1960s. However, an ecologically inflected investigation of space, time, technology and the human in Beckett's radiophonic worlds would certainly be a rewarding project. As I argue at the beginning of Section 4, Beckett continued to incorporate acousmatic sound and an intense focus on listening into his work in other media.

concept of a microcosm to the tradition of the *theatrum mundi*, however unlikely that trope may seem to Beckett's minimalist stages. Yet the *theatrum mundi* places the human in an observed arena that is simultaneously a stage, a stratified social system and, especially in medieval versions of the trope, the habitation of all earthly creatures under the benevolent or judgemental gaze of a divine being. This section briefly summarises the relevance of this trope to Beckett's early full-length plays, *Waiting for Godot* and *Endgame*, but focuses on selected mimes and abandoned dramatic fragments from the 1950s and 1960s ('Espace souterrain' / 'Coups de gong', and *Act Without Words I* and *II*), as laboratories or models for ecosystems in which humans find themselves constrained, inspected or taunted in a tightly regulated habitat.

The third section focuses on the closed space prose texts of the 1960s, though it also places these texts in the context of the relationship between the human protagonists and their environment in some of the earlier prose, and in relation to the Dante-saturated *How It Is*. The analysis focuses on *All Strange Away*, *Imagination Dead Imagine* and *The Lost Ones*, looking at how the theatrical model of a restricted and inspected place of play becomes complicated by a visual regime of perception following Beckett's work in film and television in the mid-1960s.

The fourth section examines the mediated environments of Beckett's plays for television and the televisual adaptation of the stage play *What Where*. This section considers the abstracted and meta-televisual qualities of these plays which do not feature external locations but take place within enclosed studio spaces or delimited playing areas. While all traces of living plants or animals have been erased, the world of humanly mediated 'nature' emerges through traces of Romantic literature and music, often associated with women. This section looks at the poetic quality of some of these later teleplays which attempt to wring some comfort from the ghosts of the Romantic tradition, in cases where vision is associated with longed-for apparitions or visitations rather than with inspection. Yet the desire of the dreamer for a lost other or solace constructed through these poetic and musical remains is framed as illusion. This section investigates the representation of gender as a highly acculturated sign system in these plays, and concludes with a discussion of Beckett's final play and televisual work, *What Where*, which is perhaps Beckett's most minimal evocation of an anthropocentric system destroying itself.

2 The *Theatrum Mundi* as Ecosystem: Beckett's Mimes and Dramatic Fragments

The stage has long been conceived as a model of the world and the world as a stage, exemplified by the ancient concept of the *theatrum mundi*. The origins of the trope are theological, where a divine being looks down on the actions of the world below, but, as Ruby Cohn has argued, it abounds throughout Shakespeare and Renaissance drama, and was revived in the twentieth century by Bertolt Brecht, Jean Genet, Peter Weiss and Samuel Beckett (Cohn, 1967). The concept of an enclosed environment inhabited by humans whose patterns of behaviour are scrutinised by some external observer (if not diegetically then by the reader or spectator) recurs throughout Beckett's work in different media. This section examines the concept of the *theatrum mundi* as a way of approaching Beckett's metatheatrical presentation of the stage as a place of inspection in a number of his earlier plays, mimes and dramatic fragments from the later 1940s to the 1950s. One of these fragments in particular, 'Espace souterrain', is examined as a model for the highly regulated closed spaces inhabited by human creatures that feature in the prose works of the 1960s and beyond. While Beckett's earlier drama can be linked to the *theatrum mundi* in its satirical view of human social organisation and mores, as portrayed, for example, through Winnie's futile though determined attempts to shore up middle-class etiquette and manners far from any society in *Happy Days*, his mimes in particular frequently position human figures in a spatio-temporal perspective where their activity is de-individualised, so that their position and behaviour in the overall system of their habitat is foregrounded.

Versions of the *Theatrum Mundi*

The history of the *theatrum mundi* trope constitutes a palimpsest of theological, philosophical and artistic representations of the place of the human in creation. The concept of the world as a stage on which humans act out their lives derives initially from ancient Greek philosophy: Ernst Robert Curtius' *European Literature and the Latin Middle Ages* gives an overview of how the trope evolved from its Greek origins to its re-emergence in sixteenth- and seventeenth-century Europe (Curtius, 1953). Plato describes man as a puppet of the gods which may be 'their plaything only, or created with a purpose' (2012, 167), an image then taken up in early Christianity, with Augustine declaring that 'the whole life of the human race, a life of trial and temptation, is no more than a show played out on stage' (2004, 113). As Björn Quiring argues in the introduction to a more recent survey of the concept, the *theatrum mundi* then became a frequent image in the European theatre of the sixteenth and seventeenth centuries, in works by Calderon and Shakespeare, as in the famous lines from *As You Like It*: 'All the world's a stage / And all the men and women merely players' (Shakespeare, 1986, 717). Quiring notes the ambiguity of the trope as it encompasses both divine and secular visions of the cosmos:

> On the one hand, the metaphor of the *theatrum mundi* can portray life as the constant flux of roles, players and plots, thence as contingent, frail and deceitful. On the other hand, it can lend stability to life by the idea that the fortunes of each actor derive from the power of a transcendent director and proceed according to eternally prescribed instructions. The metaphor may denigrate or elevate the world, depending on whether one likes the resultant cosmic play or not. The decisive question is whether the world-theatre is in fact limitless: is a director and some stage machinery all that exists beyond the stage itself? (Quiring, 2014, 2)

The *theatrum mundi* therefore plays on theatre's focus on the here and now (the actions of plays and players on the stage before an audience), but the trope as metaphor or allegory transforms this small bounded scene into a 'world', whether an anthropocentric comedy of manners or a tragedy of human weakness, or a perspective on the ephemerality of human affairs in the context of eternal time or timelessness.

During the Renaissance, the 'world' is frequently envisaged as a perfect system designed by the Christian God. Thomas Browne's *The Garden of Cyrus*, originally published in 1658, presents the natural world as a garden arranged by God in the shape of a quincunx.[16] Nature is portrayed here as subject to the same symmetry and order as the spheres. The figuring of the *theatrum mundi* as a chessboard in a play by Thomas Middleton, *A Game at Chess* (1624), derives from this sense of the cosmos operating according to a preordained pattern. However, such concepts of a changeless *mise en scène* whose signs can be decoded by the faithful begin to be modified by new discoveries in technology and science such as the telescope, which Galileo invented in 1601, as Beckett noted.[17] The world is no longer viewed from the stable point of view of an external creator, but through technologically enhanced and mediated human inspection, which fractures the field of vision as it magnifies a section of it. Anselm Haverkamp argues that, by the seventeenth century, 'the *theatrum mundi* had turned from a coherent allegory of divine action into a mixed metaphor of observation, a laboratory of epistemological concerns' (2014, 141). The *theatrum mundi* trope therefore combines contradictory perspectives on humans as part of a divinely ordained cosmological order, as players in a stratified social and class system, or as scientific (male, European) observers whose technologies turn the world into an object of knowledge. In each case, however, the concept implies a microcosm or delimited system which is under external inspection, observation or control. This section argues that

---

[16] See Peter Murphy (1982) on Beckett's frequent use of the quincunx image as found in Browne's *The Garden of Cyrus*.
[17] See Beckett's *Dream Notebook* (Beckett, 1999, 146).

Beckett used the theatre, especially in his mimes and abandoned dramatic fragments, to model such a precisely regulated microcosm where humans are subject to external laws (which may be internalised) determining their movement and behaviour, and to some form of inspection or surveillance.

The *Theatrum Mundi* in Beckett's Early Plays

Ruby Cohn's essay on Beckett's use of the *theatrum mundi* concept in some of the full-length plays focuses on Beckett's characters' consciousness of being observed. She comments on the continual references to the actual theatrical audience in *Endgame* as part of the play's self-conscious theatricality and artifice, implicating the audience as witness (Cohn, 1967, 30). Cohn also notes that 'sustained through most of his drama, however, is a faint recollection of the God-spectator tradition of *theatrum mundi*' (31), as in Vladimir's thought that 'At me too someone is looking' (Beckett, 1986, 84), or Winnie's comment that 'Someone is looking at me still' (160). Both of these phrases create an ambiguity about whether the gaze is from a divine or other extra-human observer or from the actual theatre audience.[18] Although *Waiting for Godot* takes place on the open road, the stage space physicalises the tramps' inability to break free of their routine of waiting for Godot. Vladimir and Estragon supposedly leave in order to find shelter during the night (though of course we do not see them leave except very briefly when Pozzo's arrival frightens them), and Pozzo and Lucky as well as the Boy come and go, but the two itinerants return day after day to the same spot (as far as they can tell). When directing *Godot* for the Schiller Theater, Beckett initially envisioned prison bars projected across the stage (Knowlson and McMillan, 1993, xxii), although he later rejected the idea as too explicit. The recognition of the stage as a playing space on which they act out their waiting is emphasised in the text by the metatheatrical references to where they are as the 'Board' (Beckett, 1986, 81) as in the phrase 'treading the boards', or to the backstage conveniences: 'end of the corridor, on the left' (35). The non-realist timing of the rising of the moon and the stylised repetition of the two acts and the movement of the tramps suggest

---

[18] Cohn does not discuss *Eleutheria*, whose publication and performing rights Beckett withdrew. The play was finally published after Beckett's death, but the performing rights remain unavailable. *Eleutheria* is a satire on the failure of middle-class society to acknowledge and take account of the horrors of World War II and its legacies, with references to barbed wire, towers, flames and ash (Blackman, 2009). Its geographical references merge specific references to Paris and places from Beckett's Irish youth (Boxall, 1998), and the play evokes less directly the *theatrum mundi* trope. However, it is highly metatheatrical (McMillan and Fehsenfeld, 1988, 29–45), including a Pirandellian figure of the Spectator who threatens to torture the main character Victor for not conforming to middle-class norms of theatrical entertainment, and it deliberately fragments and disorients the audience's observation and interpretation of what they are seeing through the device of a split stage (McMullan, 2010, 25–8).

that they are caught up and regulated by these wider systems of time, seasons and motion under (perhaps) the rather negligent responsibility of Mr Godot or some other entity. James Knowlson notes that when Beckett directed *Warten auf Godot* for the Schiller Theater in 1975, he articulated 'an elemental or cosmological set of contrasts' (Knowlson and McMillan, 1993, xiv) such as earth and sky, mineral and vegetable or horizontal and vertical. Vladimir and Estragon are not contained in an interior space, but placed on a stage-cosmos with its own mechanical moon. Seeing or being seen is a recurrent concern: Beckett's Schiller Theater directing notes list Vladimir and Estragon's 'inspection of place' (Knowlson and McMillan, 1993, 321), while they both refer to an external gaze which is desired as proof of existence or a meaningful pattern to their existence: Vladimir says to the Boy: 'You're sure you saw me' (Beckett, 1986, 86), and Estragon invokes God: 'Do you think God sees me?' (71).

In *Endgame*, Beckett develops further both the desire for and the destabilisation of human life as a coherent entity that can be chronicled or visually accessed as a whole. Martin Harries includes Beckett in what he describes as a counter-tradition within the *theatrum mundi* which specifically questions how the trope constructs the totalising concept of a 'world' available to be seen. Harries suggests that 'the problem of the occupant of [a] spectator's place, whether man or god, gets radicalised in Beckett's work' (2014, 232). Rather than the audience being privy to more information or scenes than the characters, as in much traditional drama, Beckett limits or undermines what the audience can see or interpret, and vision is often refracted and mediated. The set of *Endgame*, for example, is an enclosed interior or 'refuge' only partially visible to the audience: the kitchen is off-stage and only Clov has access to whatever can be seen out of the high windows with the aid of Galileo's 'glass' (Beckett, 1986, 105) or telescope. Clov relays his observations in words to the blind Hamm, but for the most part he asserts that there is nothing to see: 'Zero' (106).[19] Harries argues that 'if the Christian concept of the *theatrum mundi* rescued appearances by making of the visible an index of the transcendent, Beckett simultaneously debunks the notion of divine spectatorship and the notion of the wholeness of the world that it guarantees' (2014, 233). The place of God in *Endgame* seems to be absent, since the characters' prayers result in 'Nothing doing' (Beckett, 1986, 119). Hamm's attempt to imagine a hypothetical position of privileged spectatorship or totalised vision exterior to human affairs – 'if a rational being came back to earth, wouldn't he be liable to

---

[19] At one point, Clov turns the telescope onto the audience, commenting ironically, 'I see ... a multitude ... in transports ... of joy' (Beckett, 1986, 106), but, in his own productions, Beckett removed that line and other specific references to the audience in order to intensify the hermeticism of the stage world (Gontarski, 1992, 250).

get ideas into his head if he observed us long enough' (108) – rather asserts his conviction that any such overview or insight is a fantasy.

Endgame therefore stages the shift Jonathan Crary analysed in *Techniques of the Observer: On Vision and Modernity in the Nineteenth Century* (1990), from the sixteenth- and seventeenth-century European concept of an apparently autonomous vision with a clear separation between observer and observed object, modelled on the *camera obscura* but also evoking a proscenium stage, to a more physiological and subjective mode of seeing via technologies such as the stereoscope, which augments but also fractures vision. *Endgame* articulates nostalgia for the visual capture of the world associated with the perspective of the *theatrum mundi*, even as the play undermines any stability of vision, including that of the spectator.

Metatheatrical references to the stage as a playing space proliferate in *Endgame*, with many references to dialogue, asides and soliloquys. The name of the central character, Hamm, recalls not just *Hamlet* but a 'ham' actor. Beckett's 1967 comment to Haerdter during Berlin rehearsals of *Endgame* about theatre as 'a small world with its own laws' where one 'conducts the action as if upon a chessboard' (McMillan and Fehsenfeld, 1988, 231) draws attention to the overall system of the 'game' which determines individual moves, whether or not anyone is in control. As in the *theatrum mundi* trope, space and time are both confined (by the parameters of the stage) and expandable. *Endgame* continually returns to the experience of time in the present moment that the characters try to fill: 'CLOV: Keep going, can't you, keep going!' (Beckett, 1986, 122). However, the dialogue evokes a much more cosmic space-time perspective with repeated references to the 'earth', 'the universe' or 'humanity', as well as other dimensions such as the extraterrestrial viewpoint Hamm mentions or the 'other hell' beyond the walls (Beckett, 1986, 104). Although the audience cannot visually verify this, the world outside of the refuge is presented as locally or globally devastated. Though it is not entirely clear which – 'beyond the hills . . . perhaps it's still green' (111) – the many ironic references to creation in *Endgame* present a dying world whose resources and inhabitants, both human and non-human, are becoming extinct (see Lyons, 1964, and Connor, 2006).[20] Space is also protean: the refuge can become the whole world for Hamm when Clov takes him on a tour of its walls. At another point, Hamm speaks of his experience of blindness as being surrounded by 'infinite emptiness . . . all the resurrected dead of all the ages wouldn't fill it, and there you'll be like a little bit of grit in the middle of the steppe' (Beckett, 1986, 109–10).

---

[20] The two windows in *Endgame* apparently look out onto 'the earth' and 'the ocean', which, in the Bible, God divided on the third day of creation (Genesis 1:9–10).

Endgame does not just reflect on the absence of a benevolent divine creator, leaving the world to be extinguished, but on the responsibility in its decline of powerful humans such as the younger Hamm. The agency of the *anthropos* over the environment, epitomised in the famous statement by the pre-Socratic Greek philosopher Protagoras that 'man is the measure of all things',[21] has also dwindled: although, according to his chronicle, Hamm once had the instruments to measure the elements of the biosphere, referring to his thermometer (temperature), heliometer (seasons according to the sun's position), anemometer (wind) and hygrometer (humidity), in the present of the play he is reduced to micro-measuring whether his wheelchair is 'right in the centre' of the refuge (Beckett, 1986, 105). Indeed, the world evoked in *Endgame* is one where human agency is almost entirely destructive – Hamm seems to have been a powerful and privileged figure who enslaved those around him, whom he refers to as 'the creatures, the creatures' (113). He hoarded resources from food to light, to be dispensed at his whim, deciding life and death. Clov reminds Hamm that when Mother Pegg asked him for oil for her lamp 'and you told her to get out to hell, you knew what was happening then, no? You know what she died of, Mother Pegg? Of darkness' (129). However, Hamm's authority is now limited to the enclosed space of the stage, and it depends on whether the other characters, especially Clov, obey his commands. This version of the *theatrum mundi* confronts audiences with the results of millennia of human exploitation and hoarding of the earth's resources, with references to the biblical pharaohs and the Irish Famine, as well as the resonances of nuclear destruction evoked by the devastated landscape beyond the refuge.

The concern to present on stage a restricted environment in which humans and sometimes other species are regulated and observed as in the trope of the *theatrum mundi* can be traced across Beckett's early plays and recurs in many of the later ones. However, in order to focus in greater detail on the closed space motif, this section now examines the period between *Godot* and *Endgame*, when Beckett had some trouble deciding what form or direction his next play would take and he experimented with several short, often abandoned mimes or dramatic fragments. As Pim Verhulst has noted, Beckett experienced a 'growing sense of writer's block in the early 1950s' (2015, 149), after the 'frenzy of writing' in French in the late 1940s following his return to Paris. This highly productive period saw Beckett composing both prose – the *Nouvelles / Novellas* ('Premier amour' / 'First Love', 'L'Expulsé / 'The Expelled', 'Le Calmant' / 'The Calmative' and 'La Fin' / 'The End'), *Mercier et Camier / Mercier and Camier*,

---

[21] Beckett includes this phrase in the notes he made from his readings in philosophy during the 1930s, now held in the Trinity College Dublin Library (TCD MS 10967/44).

Molloy, Malone meurt / Malone Dies and *L'Innommable / The Unnamable* –
and drama, in the two plays for theatre *Eleutheria* and *En attendant Godot*.
Beckett had completed *L'Innommable* in 1950 and the *Textes pour rien / Texts
for Nothing* in 1950–1: there would not be a further major prose work until
Comment c'est / How It Is, written between 1958 and 1960 (Pilling, 2006,
143–9). Unable to make headway in prose, Beckett launched into the first
drafts of what would finally emerge as *Fin de partie / Endgame*, but the
genesis of this play, unlike *Godot*, which was written very quickly, would be
extremely laborious as it went through many versions and drafts until final
completion in 1956.[22] The published mimes date from around 1955 for *Act
Without Words I* and 1958/9 for *Act Without Words II*, but the early drafts of
Fin de partie and other fragments include wordless movement sequences.
Stan Gontarski argues that:

> [Beckett's] experiments with wordless drama opened up possibilities that
> were realised in the drama of the fifties. [...] Beckett was not quite writing
> a sequence of plays, but he seems to have been preoccupied with the mime
> genre and a series of themes appear, disappear and reappear in various guises
> within the plays of this period. (1985, 25–6)

The next section argues that these short mimes or fragments model versions
of strictly regulated hermetic environments that would continue to impact on
Beckett's work across different media for decades to come. In fact, the abandoned work I begin with is a hybrid genre like several of the dramatic fragments
that Beckett was working on at this time, including the *Endgame* drafts – he
would start with a mimed scenario and then include passages of monologue or
dialogue. As in the *theatrum mundi*, humans are placed in a micro-environment
or theatrical ecosystem in order to be observed.

'Espace souterrain' / 'Coups de gong' as Model for Beckett's Closed Space Systems

This unpublished dramatic fragment has two versions: the first one, 'Espace
souterrain' ('Underground Space'), is dated June 1952, and the second one,
'Coups de gong' ('Gong Strikes'), is undated.[23] Both were written in French as
was most of Beckett's writing at this time. The first of the two manuscripts,
which consists of eleven handwritten pages, envisages the setting and the

---

[22] See Dirk Van Hulle and Shane Weller (2018) for a detailed analysis of the genetic history of *Fin
de partie / Endgame*, including a discussion of some elements that 'Espace souterrain' and
'Coups de gong' have in common with the earliest manuscripts in the genetic sequence.

[23] Both manuscripts are held in the University of Reading Beckett Collection: 'Espace souterrain'
UoR MS 2931 and 'Coups de gong' UoR MS 2932. These manuscripts are briefly discussed in
Nixon (2014, 290–1) and Van Hulle and Weller (2018, 141–2).

action. With the exception of the name 'Camier' (from Beckett's novel *Mercier and Camier*), the human figures are not named but given letters from A to Y (not Z interestingly), suggesting a long series. It is in Beckett's typically illegible scrawl – parts of it are quite indecipherable. The second version is a three-page typescript which has the same scenario with very minor changes – fewer figures and more dialogue – there is just a fragment of dialogue in the first manuscript.

The scenario in 'Espace souterrain' involves a repeated cycle of interlinked actions where one group of figures disappears into individual holes in the ground, accompanied by the sound of a gong, while another group, each of whom has come to look for someone from the first group, leans over them as they disappear and they in turn, tied to their sinking partner by a rope around their necks, begin to sink into the same hole. Meanwhile, a further group descends from rope ladders hung from the flies which are then pulled up again, in order to search for their lost ones, in a series that is noted as being potentially infinite. The stage directions indicate that the one who descends always arrives too late (presumably to see or save the disappearing one). The manuscript also divides these figures into '*chercheurs*' and '*cherchés*' – searchers and sought – anticipating the searchers of *Le Dépeupleur* / *The Lost Ones* of more than a decade later. There is also a specific reference to that title, taken from the Lamartine line 'un seul être vous manque et tout est dépeuplé' ('you miss one person and the world is empty') in the first manuscript (Lamartine, 2005, 71): the directions announce that the upper space is increasingly emptied of people.

The next version, beginning 'Coups de gong', is a more condensed version of this system with four named figures: L'Englouti, as his name suggests (from the French verb *engloutir*, to be swallowed up or engulfed), is already half sunk into the ground; L'Anonyme (Anonymous) is bending over him as he disappears; in the other hole, Camier is bending over an already empty hole (seeking Mercier?): he will start sinking into the hole during the piece which ends when Camier has sunk to his waist, mirroring the position of L'Englouti at the opening (in the first version, the play begins and ends when only the head of each is still visible). There is also another group of figures, who seem to be officials of some sort, and in the typescript one of these is named as L'Envoyé, the envoy, who arrives from the ladder carrying some rope and who, unlike the searchers and the disappeared, can come and go (he exits by the stage wings, not the ladders). The searchers are dressed in long, whitish nightgowns trailing on the floor and are wearing medals which the envoy inspects. However, in the typescript, L'Anonyme, who is tied to L'Englouti by a rope and is evidently the next in line to disappear, manages to get free, and the last section of the manuscript is his monologue in which he contemplates his life now that he is free to come and go. Yet, like Victor in Beckett's first full-length play, *Eleutheria*, L'Anonyme muses that he will neither go nor come. While this figure has been liberated from the mechanism of engulfment since he has escaped being dragged into the hole, he seems to remain confined psychologically (he will not leave), suggesting an internalisation of the system. 'Espace souterrain' / 'Coups de gong' maintains an ambiguity as to who or what controls the system, though the first version mentions a sort of permanent organisation, linking the fragment to preoccupations about surveillance and incarceration in Beckett's post–World War II writing.[24] Emilie Morin reminds us of the many 'allusions to disappearances and conspiracies masterminded by unnamed powers and institutions' in *Molloy* and *Malone Dies*, for example (2017, 173), which are recalled in these dramatic fragments from the early 1950s.

The fragments are intriguing for many reasons. They look back to the preoccupations of earlier work and anticipate future work: the sets of figures can be related to the series of pseudo-couples that recur in Beckett's work of the post–World War II era such as Mercier and Camier or Didi and Gogo. The rope motif recalls Lucky who is tied to Pozzo by a rope in *Godot*, and the figure submerged up to the waist and sinking further prefigures Winnie in *Happy Days*. The underground space anticipates the many infernal or purgatorial spaces in future work, and includes some of the specific Dantean references that will feature again in the novel *How It is*, explored in the next section. *The Inferno* frequently refers to bodies sinking into holes, as in Canto VII, where the sullen are submerged in the slime of the Styx. In Canto XIX in particular, the mud is perforated with round holes in which sinners are piled on top of each other, with their feet protruding into the air, scorched by flames. Dante recognises Pope Nicholas, who mistakes him for the still alive Pope Boniface. Nicholas is expecting Boniface to join him in the same hole, and then another to come after him in turn, as in the rota of sinking into the ground in 'Espace souterrain'.[25] However, I want to focus in the next section on the role of mime, or wordless drama sequences, as models for a contained environment using, as in the *theatrum mundi* trope, the mechanics and spatial qualities of the stage (with its offstage wings, flies and so on) as an entire world within which a series of human figures perform repeated and regulated movement patterns. I conclude by looking briefly at the persistence of traces of this trope in Beckett's later stage plays.

---

[24] Nixon notes that the dramatic fragment follows some of the prose texts that Beckett had abandoned, including 'On le tortura bien' and 'Ici personne ne vient jamais', the latter in particular described as a 'transitional' text which 'anticipates Beckett's "closed space" fiction of the next twenty years' (2014, 290).

[25] The merging of an ecological, political and infernal landscape of extermination is prefigured in the Molloy country, where, between his home town and the sea, there is a 'stinking, steaming swamp in which an incalculable number of human lives were yearly engulfed' (Beckett, 1976, 70).

Beckett's Mimes and Fragments: The Stage as Regulated Habitat

Mime dispenses with dialogue or monologue, reducing individual psychology or subjective viewpoint in order to foreground an image of the human condition articulated through a non-psychologised poetic of the body of the performer in relation to other bodies or objects within the space of the stage.[26] Most of Beckett's mimes portray the human body as subject to an environment whose mechanisms are externally controlled and within which they have very limited agency. The two itinerant figures in *Act Without Words II* are prompted out of their sacks into their daily routine by a goad and then carry each other across the stage in a series of repeated, interdependent actions that recall the interdependent pairs of 'Espace souterrain'. Beckett included repeated mime sequences at the beginning of *Endgame* and *Krapp's Last Tape* portraying human action as regulated rather than a spontaneous expression of an autonomous subject. Other mimes such as the later televisual mime *Quad* or the stage version of *What Where* include this sense of serial patterning, which also suggests some externally or internally driven mechanism determining the human figures.

The personae of Beckett's mimes are therefore far from self-determining, autonomous and sovereign subjects. Several scholars have noted Beckett's interest in Wolfgang Köhler's *The Mentality of Apes* ([1917] 1927), resulting from research into the behaviour of chimpanzees in captivity. Köhler deduced that the chimpanzees were indeed capable of some cognition, challenging any absolute distinction between human and other animals. Ulrika Maude notes Beckett's references to Darwinian evolutionary theory and his awareness of the debates of the early twentieth century into the 'dichotomy between conceptual and biomechanical models of cognition and behaviour' and the 'repeated subjection of his characters to stimulus-response experiments' (2013, 85).[27] Indeed Shane Weller comments that *Act Without Words I*, informed by Köhler's experiments with animals, exposes the manipulation and violence behind such subjection to behavioural experiments by presenting the specimen whose behaviour is being observed (by the audience) as human: 'the very attempt to determine whether the ape possesses "genuine intelligence" becomes a mode of torture' (2008, 216). Beckett here subjects his human figure to the kind of technologies of observation and control of other species characteristic of

---

[26] Beckett would have encountered an experimental mime tradition through Jean-Louis Barrault, who had trained with Étienne Decroux, who had trained in turn with Jacques Copeau in *mime corporel*, and through Roger Blin, who had studied mime with Barrault (see McMullan, 2010, 57–8). Knowlson has also noted Beckett's interest in marionettes and the theories of von Kleist and Edward Gordon Craig: see Knowlson and Pilling (1979, 277–85) and Tucker (2015).

[27] See also Tajiri (2013).

anthropocentric systems of science and knowledge. But Beckett's mime laboratory is also a theatre, in the artistic as well as scientific sense.

Beckett's mimes often overtly exploit the actual architecture of the stage in order to present in a concrete experiential way the spatial and behavioural constraints on the bodies of the actor-figures. 'Espace souterrain' draws attention to the axes of the stage space: to the ladders descending and ascending from the flies and the holes or trapdoors into which the figures sink below stage level, as well as to the offstage wings from which L'Envoyé enters and exits. The man in *Act Without Words I* is taunted by various aids to survival in his desert landscape that are lowered from the flies and then withdrawn by some unseen force before they can be grasped, so that he finally retreats within himself, staring at his useless hands which are normally a prime agent of human instrumental action on the external world. Jürgen Siess notes that *Act Without Words I* foregrounds the mechanisms and the creative and technical agents of the theatre itself:

> The persona signifies the actor depending on the machinery, actually on the agents operating above or behind the scene and ultimately depending on the director. If one agrees that *Act Without Words I* is just theatre, the conclusion will be that the manipulation in the theatre production system is *shown* as such. (Siess, 2003, 300; italics in original)

The audience members are therefore also subject to and part of the operating conditions of the theatre insofar as they fulfil their role as observers. *Happy Days* acknowledges this by having Winnie woken by a bell, like the bell in a theatre summoning the audience members to their seats.[28] Beckett's dramatic works therefore invite the spectators to reflect on their role as both external observers activating the mechanisms which regulate the onstage bodies, and as subjects of those mechanisms and the behavioural, perceptual and sensory conditions of the drama's ecosystem. Carl Lavery argues that it is in this sense that Beckett's theatre 'weathers' its audience, so that we experience 'a different rhythm, in which humans and non-humans are caught in the vast and paradoxical endlessness of time's eternal transience'. By defamiliarising and recalibrating our experience of time in particular, 'where we are undone in and by time, deposed and dispossessed on the earth, Beckett's theatre leaves us as helpless and indeterminate "as a little bit of grit in the middle of the steppe"[29] that knows not where its future will be' (Lavery, 2018a, 25).

Beckett's mimes are also concerned with the dimensions of time and space so evident in *Endgame*. 'Espace souterrain' emphasises both the constraints of the

---

[28] See Pattie (2018, 232): 'In the theatre, the coercive system exists outside of the text – in the mechanisms of the theatre itself.'

[29] The quotation is from *Endgame* (Beckett, 1986, 110).

stage apparatus and a circular, repetitive, potentially infinite time frame beyond the horizon of any individual life. This becomes the central concern of the Petit Odéon dramatic fragments from the later 1960s which, though not a closed space text, are concerned with contrasting spatial and temporal perspectives.[30] In a letter to Ruby Cohn on 30 January 1967, Beckett writes that he is looking for 'a way of reducing stage time as one can stage space'.[31] The female speaker measures out her life and that of her male partner in doses of two liquids, one a tranquiliser and the other an energiser. She calculates that the remaining amount will give them 125,000 hours of life, or about fourteen years. Yet, in another section of the monologue, this measured time is contrasted with the immense and unlimited vistas of their last journey together through a landscape scattered with the bones of enormous animals, perhaps those of elephants or mammoths, evoking a pre- or post-human landscape and temporality.[32] Beckett's versions of the *theatrum mundi* as theatre laboratories both place human specimens under observation in the here and now of the stage environment, and evoke spatial and temporal perspectives which reduce human lives and histories to an infinite procession of interdependent bodies subjected to an externally imposed framework, whether technical, human or divine/infernal. Withholding the interior perspective of the personae's thoughts and feelings in the mimes places the emphasis on the overarching system of their habitat. Yet Beckett returns to the interior articulation of human subjectivity through speech in some of these fragments, expressing an awareness on the part of the figures that, given the conditions of their existence, their options are limited. On one hand, as mentioned earlier in this Element, we might read this as the internalisation of a political or representational system that shapes human subject-ivity and action, or, on the other, as a recognition that humans are not always in control of their and others' destinies. Beckett thereby, as Lavery argues, forges new affective and conceptual paradigms in 'an alternative kind of eco-practice, rooted in a recognition of limits and capacities' (Lavery, 2018b, 4).

Traces of the *Theatrum Mundi* as Staged Ecosystem in Beckett's Later Work

Quiring suggests that, since Descartes, 'the metaphor of the *theatrum mundi* becomes replaced and neutralised by the *topos* of the mind as the space that is truly able to represent the world' (2014, 12–13). Beckett's later prose work

---

[30] UoR MS 1227/7/16/3 and MS 2927.

[31] UoR MS 5100, COH/27; qtd. in McMullan (2010, 66).

[32] Chris Ackerley has traced Beckett's juxtaposition between the anthropocentric timescale of the history of human thought, science and activities, and the more-than-human scale of geological time, to a 1938 poem, 'ainsi a-t-on beau': 'a poem in which human awareness is set against past eras, the age of mammoths and the dinotherium, ice-ages that brought nothing new (only humanity)' (Ackerley, 2005, 70).

confirms this interiorisation of the trope in the recurrent motif of fictional worlds explicitly conjured by the imagination of the author-creator. In these texts, considered in the next section, any recognisably mimetic exterior setting has been erased, but the enclosed fictional worlds are still constructed in order to be observed and indeed measured. The later drama, from *Play* onwards, is likewise divested of any exterior location, and the tightly focused visual image is outlined against darkness, creating an ambiguity as to whether this space represents the mind or memory of the speaker(s), one or more fictional locations (both the interior of the childhood home and the church through which May paces in *Footfalls*, for example), or the stage itself.

Play, a transitional dramatic text in Beckett's presentation of stage worlds alienated from the world 'in the sun' (1986, 315), presents an even more condensed version of the mechanised system of many of the mimes. Although the stage is shrouded in darkness which seems limitless, the three heads in their urns are entirely immobile, and their existence consists purely of their enforced responses to the Light which elicits fragments of a narrative of a banal middle-class *ménage à trois* followed by their experience of being under the Light's interrogation. It is unclear what the Light represents, whether an externalisation of the psyche of one or all of the figures, some infernal, purgatorial or divine instrument of judgement or torture, or an entirely mechanical function operating randomly. It uses the technologies of the theatre, especially the spotlight, and anchors the actors' bodies in urns on stage, to concretise their imprisonment within the system the play sets up (as its title suggests), as well as invoking scenarios of witnessing, interrogation and judgement.

Following *Play*, the space of the stage increasingly seems to materialise the interior of someone's mind or memory, and though these speakers all desire to be seen and heard, the focus is often on the fracturing of the individual subject amongst the imagining mind and its figments, including its figments of self. Unlike *The Unnamable*, however, which also inhabits this interiorised space, the theatre from *Not I* to *Rockaby* focuses on the visible space of the stage as inhabited both by the material body of the actor and by the body or body part of the persona as an imagined semblance: the embodied subject imagining its embodiments (see McMullan, 2010). These short dramas take a less objectified view of their subjects, and their affective power derives at least partly from their articulation of loss and marginalisation in the public space of the stage. Whether male or female, many of them offer a profoundly alienated perspective on a world dominated by human assumptions of status, respectability or techno-logical advancement, whether that of Mouth, who narrates the isolation of 'she' in the supermarket or in court, or the two old men from another century by the side of a busy road assaulted by the sounds of the modern world in *The Old Tune*

(1963), Beckett's translation of Robert Pinget's *La Manivelle*. Yet the *theatrum mundi* re-emerges again in plays from the very last years of Beckett's writing career: *Catastrophe* – where the actual audience in the theatre is doubled by the fictional audience of the play who applaud the image of destitute humanity crafted from the live body of the silent Protagonist by an authoritarian director and his Assistant before the eyes of the actual audience – and *What Where*, discussed in Section 4. In between, my contention is that the concept of the closed system which can be related to the *theatrum mundi* mutated across media and re-emerged in the prose works of the 1960s and the teleplays of the subsequent decades, including the mime for television *Quad*, explored in Section 4.

This section has centred on 'Espace souterrain' as a *visual and kinaesthetic sketch or animated model box* of an underground highly systematised space in which a series of human figures are entrapped within the stage's own machinery. Although the underground space of this fragment is not in fact hermetic, since L'Envoyé can come and go, there is no exit for those subject to its mechanisms. The next section explores how this theatrical model is taken up and transformed into the complex textual fabric of the closed space prose narratives, which invoke continually shifting perspectives that take place within the reader's imagination.

3 Exhausted Biospheres and Techniques of Observation: The Closed Space Prose Texts

This section focuses on a series of prose texts, from *Comment c'est / How It Is*, written at the end of the 1950s, to *Le Dépeupleur / The Lost Ones*, completed in 1970, that are set in fictional environments sealed off from the earth's sunlight or stars, inhabited by only one species, the human. In many of these texts from the 1960s, the narrative evokes human bodies placed in confined spaces, inspected and measured in precise detail. The narratives position the reader as sharing this objectifying gaze, which Jonathan Crary has associated with the increased development of disciplinary technologies of observation such as the stereoscope during the nineteenth century (Crary, 1990). As these technologies relocate vision 'to a plane severed from a human observer' (1) and from 'any reference to the position of an observer in a "real", optically observed world' (2), Crary argues that such a dislocation of the model of vision which assumed a stable view of the external world by the observer produced 'a process of subjectification in which the subject is simultaneously the object of knowledge and the object of procedures of control and normalization' (92). The constant preoccupation with eyes and inspection, combined with the dislocation of a stable point of observation in many of these closed space prose texts, echoes such regulatory techniques of inspection alongside an increasing sense of both narrator and reader being subjected to the generative mechanisms of the textual world. These texts test the reader's ethical and conceptual response to a mode of inspection that combines an unsettlingly relentless, ungrounded, possibly post-human narrative perspective, like that of an indifferent creator or self-operating machine, with a pseudo-anthropological gaze turned on human specimens, in some cases the last of their species, and the conditions of their enclosed habitats.

However, before turning to these texts, I want to trace the development in Beckett's prose of the narrative depiction of what I am calling ecosystems, where the focus is not on action, dialogue, character or internal thought processes, but on the self-conscious creation of a 'small world with its own laws', in Beckett's theatrical metaphor, inhabited by a 'little people' as in *The Lost Ones*, or indeed by just one or two bodies. Although adopting a chronological approach to Beckett's composition in any medium needs to take account of the impact of works composed in other media, translations and the frequent recycling of earlier abandoned texts, certain preoccupations can nevertheless be traced across clusters of texts, including across media. Very broadly speaking, and with many detours, a discernible shift in narrative voice and fictional world is evoked in Beckett's prose from the early, densely allusive stories in *More Pricks Than Kicks* (from the early 1930s), acerbic in their social satire, to the wanderings of *Mercier and Camier* in the immediate post–World War II writing, to the retreat into a hermetic inner skull-scape and first-person narrative voice in the *Unnamable* and *Texts for Nothing* in the period from 1949 to the early 1950s. In turn, the closed space texts of the 1960s eschew this first-person narrative voice, and the space is less an interior mind space than a biosphere with its own lighting and temperature systems.

These broad shifts also entail the radical shrinking or erasure of the earthly environment of skies, clouds, sunlight or rain, fields, woods, water, mountains, animals, birds and insects, all of which feature abundantly in Beckett's pre-1960s prose (see Bryden, 2013). Beckett's earliest prose stories and novels are mainly, though not exclusively, set in urban locations, though the rural environs of Dublin in particular are evoked throughout *More Pricks Than Kicks*, culled from Beckett's first novel, *Dream of Fair to Middling Women*, unpublished during Beckett's lifetime. Nevertheless, the 'scene' the narrator depicts is often presented in anthropocentric terms, through visual or literary tropes: the 'Homer dusk' (Beckett, 1983, 197) or 'mountains swarthy Uccello' (195) of the short story 'Yellow', for example. These stories can be placed in a tradition of comedy of manners, where human characters, behaviour and social convention and interaction are satirised and the narrative is often highly self-conscious. Already in *Murphy*, however, Beckett's first novel to be published (in 1938), there is a specific juxtaposition between the outer world, whether urban or rural, and the interior space of the protagonist's psyche. Murphy's mind is described as a 'closed system [. . .] that pictured itself as a sphere full of light fading into dark', with distinct zones ranging from that in the light made up of 'forms with parallel [. . .] the elements of physical experience available for a new arrangement', to the half-light zone of 'forms without parallel' to the dynamic 'flux of forms' in the third zone of darkness (Beckett, 1973, 64). Based on 'a score of conversations [with Beckett] in 1961–2, and 1964–5' (Harvey, 1970, xii), Lawrence Harvey argues that, like Murphy's mind, Beckett's perception of the world and art 'divides the world into an upper zone of light where forms correspond to those in the physical world outside and a lower zone of darkness without such correspondence' (436). This juxtaposition between glimpses of the world 'above in the light' which indeed evoke a recognisable world, and a different order of creation which does not resemble the physical macrocosm but is subject to its own conditions and modes of generation, recurs throughout the closed space texts. While the theatre is arguably a model for the presentation of bodies in a confined space, as argued in the previous section, the prose work of the mid-1960s also incorporates references to visual technologies (such as a camera) to narrate the conditions endured by its regulated bodies, and indeed to introduce dislocations and instabilities into its own accounts.

The movement to an interior space closed off from the world of daylight was already taking place during the writing of *Molloy* in the late 1940s, which famously begins: 'I am in my mother's room' (Beckett, 1976, 9) and includes reference to the mind or imagination as a 'sealed jar' (46), but also describes the narrator's exterior journeys through the Molloy country to reach his mother's room. *The Unnamable* and the *Texts for Nothing* also alternate between external scenes and a hermetic, interior mind space from which the narrator speaks, and where every scene, story, body and identity is likely to dissolve back into an unstoppable flow or flux of words. Frequently in the *Texts for Nothing*, from their 'den' in the 'hole the centuries have dug' (Beckett, 1995, 101), the narrator imagines the world above not so much as a specific location but as the entire planet earth, perhaps simply a myth. In Text V the narrator recalls 'the sky and earth, I've heard great accounts of them' (118), and in Text VI the narrator anticipates telling 'a little story, with living creatures coming and going on a habitable earth, crammed with the dead' (126). There is a tendency therefore to refer to the earth as a cosmological system, viewed as if from the perspective of space, or an extraterrestrial or extra-temporal visitor – Hamm's 'rational being' having come 'back to earth' (Beckett, 1986, 108; see Section 2). The concern with the depiction of time and space recurs throughout these prose texts concerned with confinement, as in Text VIII: 'Time has turned into space, and there'll be no more time till I get out of here' (Beckett, 1995, 132). *How It Is* is pivotal or transitional in this narratorial shift and the presentation of the world of the novel as a dystopian cosmic system: though the narrative of *How It Is* is told in the first person, it is distanced to a certain extent by being reportedly sourced from a voice whose origin is unclear: 'I say it as I hear it' (Beckett, 1964, 7). Moreover, *How It Is* expands in much greater detail the underground landscape of the fragment 'Espace souterrain', including the pervasive references to Dante's *Inferno*.

As many scholars have pointed out, Dante is a recurrent reference point throughout Beckett's work and especially in *How It Is*, which features the tale of a naked, unnamed narrator-protagonist crawling through mud, as murmured by a voice which may be internal to the narrator, or an exterior 'ancient voice' (Beckett, 1964, 7) that he hears, or produced by Pim or the narrator through physical extortion. This featureless slime has no boundaries, but the narrative voice proposes that he and others might be moving in a straight line from left to right or from west to east, and, in Part III, in a 'closed curve' (Beckett, 1964, 127) echoing Dante's descending circles. In *Beckett's Dantes*, Daniela Caselli details the parallels between the landscape of *How It Is* and Dante's *Inferno*: 'The mud in *How It Is* is at once what permits the passing on of the murmuring and what hinders it, thus reproducing the situation of the slothful damned of the fifth circle, doomed to sing their almost unintelligible "hymn" of damnation' (Caselli, 2005, 5). The novel includes Dantean references to 'mute screams abandon hope' (Beckett, 1964, 52) and to an underground orientation in relation to the world 'above in the light' (8). It is structured in three parts, 'Before Pim', 'With Pim' and 'After Pim', echoing the division of Dante's *Divine Comedy* into Hell, Purgatory and Paradise. However, Dante's journey of salvation and absolution from Hell to Paradise as led by Virgil and then by the angelic figure of Beatrice is denied the narrator in *How It Is*. In the last part of the novel, the single narrator becomes one of a multitude of naked (male) bodies all following the same trajectory of journeying alone, meeting another, torturing him into speech and then abandoning him, only to couple with another and be tortured and abandoned in turn, just as the searcher in 'Espace souterrain' takes the place of the disappeared. The system of regulated disappearance in 'Coups de gong', described by L'Anonyme as a form of justice, is reprised in the deeply ironic references to justice in *How It Is* as constituted by an equal rotation of the roles of tortured and torturer: 'Because of our justice [. . .] not a single one of us be wronged not one deprived of tormentor as number 1 would be not one deprived of victim' (Beckett, 1964, 134). Unlike in the *Commedia*, in *How It Is*, there is no way out back to the stars as at the end of the *Inferno*, or any glimpse of the light of paradise.

However, Caselli emphasises that Beckett's intertextual references to Dante are always complex and raise questions about Beckett's use of such references as part of his own creative process rather than providing any key.[33] Anthony Cordingley has analysed the genetic composition and the texture of multiple layers of allusion in *How It Is*. He notes that, in early drafts, the narrator is in a wilderness rather than in an underground landscape, but Beckett then reread the *Inferno* during the writing process (having reread the *Paradiso* before beginning the novel), which evidently shaped the spatio-temporal location of the published novel (Cordingley, 2018, 17–19). He notes the references to Lucifer's thighs in the Inferno up which Dante and Virgil climb to exit the Inferno, which Beckett internalises into a 'digestive economy' (28), through which the narrator and others are crawling as if in some immense body: 'We are talking of a procession advancing in jerks or spasms like shit in the guts till one wonders days of great gaiety if we shall not end one after another or two by two by being shat into the open air the light of day the regimen of grace' (Beckett, 1964, 135). Cordingley also traces the multiple references to diverse abstract systems of knowledge from 'Plato, Aristotle and perhaps the Stoics, into the great natural and metaphysical systems of the 17th century' in order to figure out the 'cosmological model for God's harmonious distribution of justice' (2018, 33). Body and cosmos and interior and exterior spaces become versions or inversions of each other.

Ultimately, these models produce a profoundly satirical and dysfunctional view of the 'natural order' of both harmony and justice, so that the operation of these systems, like other cosmologies in the closed space texts, produces an oppressive system of laws (masquerading as justice) to which the bodies of their human inhabitants are subjected. Since language itself is the medium through which these systems are articulated in the narrative, *How It Is* conceives of speech as learned and produced through a repeated routine of physical torture: 'table of basic stimuli one sing nails in armpit two speak blade in arse three stop thump on skull four louder pestle in kidney' (Beckett, 1964, 76). The novel continually shifts perspective in time and space, from the intimate scenes of the narrator crawling through the excremental mud or clasped to Pim in their mutual struggle towards vocal expression, to the epic visions of multitudes of couples in endless time and space in Part III. Yet towards the end of the novel, the narrative voice suggests that the landscape, the procession of bodies and the positing of an originary or controlling entity which is 'not one of us an

---

[33] 'Intertexts in Beckett do not work as the missing piece of the puzzle able to provide us with the complete picture. In an oeuvre which asks where meanings come from and how they come about, sources will not restore an allegedly desirable full meaning; what they can do, however, is to raise important questions about how meanings take shape in Beckett' (Caselli, 2005, 6).

intelligence somewhere' (150) have all been imagined 'within in the little vault empty closed eight planes bone-white' (140), recalling the 'wombtomb' or skull spaces of the earlier prose. The space-time world of *How It Is* is therefore protean: on one hand, it is confined in terms of the linear procession through the mud, but, on the other, it opens up into 'a vast stretch of eternity' (113) and then shrinks to an interior 'vault' where images and narratives dissolve into 'a gibberish garbled sixfold' (146). Cordingley argues that the end of the novel returns to its beginning (like Joyce's *Finnegans Wake*), transforming the linear trajectory of the narrative into a circle, as the apparent linear temporality of 'Before Pim', 'With Pim' and 'After Pim' dissolves into an immense circularity of repetition containing countless other torturers and tortured. The very co-ordinates of time and space in relation to the body of self and other have been recalibrated in this alternative world of words transcribing a babble of ancient voices materialised as the mud which the narrator swallows:

> In shaping the novel into a circle, Beckett delivers an image of undefined time within its hermetic covers. Like the rotating heavens, lacking any established point of reference, the novel is its own material universe. (Cordingley, 2018, 95)

How It Is therefore picks up on a number of features of the earlier dramatic fragment 'Espace souterrain', including the references to a Dantean cosmology with the narrated or dramatised scene set underground, and a rigid, schematised system of justice that binds couples to each other. But *How It Is* is also an extraordinarily complex and innovative narrative articulation of a world both spatially confined and endless, in a temporality equally infinite yet looped. All attempts to map space and time, or the system which governs this world and its regime of corporeal discipline which the narrator has learned to call justice, ultimately collapse into the final scene of bodily torture through which the narrator/Pim screams his 'story', which we realise, as at the end of Proust's *À la Recherche du temps perdu*, is the very one we have been reading. *How It Is* presents a world governed by a disciplinary system whose agent or origin is unclear but which produces speech/language and subjectivity itself through subjection to its implacable rules.

The theatrical model of the earlier fragment is therefore taken up and transformed into the complex textual fabric and 'vast tracts of time' of the prose narrative of *How It Is* (Beckett, 1964, 7). However, both theatrical and indeed filmic modes of perception are invoked, especially in Part I of the text: the mud parts like a theatrical curtain but also a screen opening up.[34] Prior to the first image appearing, other mediating perceptual frames are invoked through which the narrative figure

---

[34] See Paraskeva (2017) for the pervasive influence of cinema and the intermedial interchanges between theatre and cinema throughout Beckett's work.

conjured by the voice inspects the other (or self as other): 'some creature or other I watched him after my fashion from afar through my spy-glass sidelong in mirrors through windows at night first image' (Beckett, 1964, 9). The narrative point of view continues to change from the visual images of a specific life in Part I juxtaposed with 'vast tracts of time' and human endeavour, to the haptic, viscerally embodied descriptions of the violent, coercive training of Pim to tell his story and sing in Part II, to the evocations of thousands or millions of bodies coupling and separating in Part III in an epic 'scale of magnitude' (113), before dissolving back into the narrative voice as dialogue produced through the infliction of pain: 'my voice yes mine yes not another's no mine alone yes sure yes a few scraps yes that no one hears no but less and less no answer LESS AND LESS yes' (160).

Although *How It Is*, like many of the closed space texts of the 1960s, rarely features any species other than the human in the mudscape, the concern with 'species' recurs throughout the novel. Cordingley notes the Platonic references embedded in the recurrent concern with species, evoking the generic model from which particular forms derive (2018, 83), relating the individual to an overarching pattern or system which is in crisis – the novel's narrator refers to 'loss of species' (Beckett, 1964, 29) or being 'never quite fallen from my species' (138). However, this continual reference to 'the species the human' (52) also carries taxonomic resonances where, rather than being the one who names all the other species (like Adam), 'man' is being named and described. *How It Is*, like many of the later closed space texts, casts the human as a species viewed from a non-anthropocentric spatio-temporal perspective. We have seen that *How It Is* invokes diverse modes of visual mediation in its narrative, including both theatre and cinematic references. However, Beckett's world-making in the narrative mode seems to have been significantly impacted by his experience of working with the visual medium of film, after Barney Rosset invited him to write a film script and he was involved in the filming of *Film* in New York in 1964. Scholars have also discussed the importance of Beckett's collaboration with French filmmaker and producer Marin Karmitz on the film of Jean-Marie Serreau's stage version of *Comédie* in 1965.[35] While the closed space texts of the 1960s focus on a body in a confined space which recalls the 'spatial art of the theatre' (Little, 2020, 89), the sense of visual inspection and observation also evokes technologies of observation, including the camera.

The Turn to the 'Eye of Prey' in the 1960s

Beckett's prose of the mid-1960s overtly charts a compositional shift from his narratives of endless journeying or displacement (even through the subterranean

---

[35] See Herren (2009), Foster (2012) and Paraskeva (2017, 67–71).

mud of *How It Is*) to the largely visual focus on a figure or figures in a cramped space.[36] The beginning of *All Strange Away* overtly signals this change:

> Out of the door and down the road in the old hat and coat like after the war, no, not that again. Five foot square, six high, no way in, none out, try for him there. (Beckett, 1995, 169)

All Strange Away is part of a cluster of prose texts that construct a world where an exhausted imagination traps the human figure under an optical lens in a relentless glare of light.[37] These closed spaces combine qualities of interior space with the sense of a cosmological or ecological system: *All Strange Away*'s 'Same system light and heat with sweat more or less, cringing away from walls, burning soles, now one, now the other' (Beckett, 1995, 171); the 'passage from heat and light to black and cold' (183) of *Imagination Dead Imagine*, or the oscillation of the temperature between hot and cold in *The Lost Ones*. These closed space texts of the 1960s are also presented as self-consciously 'imagined': Gontarski notes that 'the mysterious narrator is often recorded in the midst of the fiction making process' (2017, 58).

The earlier prose contains traces of this self-conscious medium-specific act of composition, but the work in audiovisual media of the later 1950s and early 1960s seems to have transformed the concept of composition or creation in the prose texts from that of the *Unnamable*'s textual autogenesis – making himself up from words or stories or from a voice that may be within or without – into a stage or screen, where the act of imagination opens up 'a space, then someone in it, that again' (Beckett, 1995, 169), a motif that recurs again and again in the prose texts. In *Beckett, Modernism and the Material Imagination*, Steven Connor argues:

> Thinking about the nature of finitude in Beckett's work often centres on the faculty he calls the 'imagination' which alternates between the visionary inheritance of Romanticism and a much more limited, often almost mechanical, faculty conceived as the power of forming images. For Beckett, imagination is not a spontaneously indwelling and upwelling power, but a strenuous and exhausting labour that comes close to the ideas of staging, seeing through or putting into practice. (2014, 7)

The self-conscious imaginative construction of the image and the focus on visual observation in these closed space texts evoke not only the stage but

---

[36] The phrase 'eye of prey' recurs in Beckett's work; see the end of *Imagination Dead Imagine*: 'at the same instant for the eye of prey the infinitesimal shudder instantly suppressed' (Beckett, 1995, 185).

[37] Paul Davies suggests that Beckett's later prose 'sets the planetary biosphere directly at odds with the environment of the artificial interior' (2006, 72).

screen-based media, or indeed other optical techniques of scientific examin-
ation. The narrator in *Imagination Dead Imagine* precisely describes the two
white bodies enclosed in their white rotunda: 'With their left hands they hold
their left legs a little below the knee, with their right hands their left arms a little
above the elbow. In this agitated light, its great white calm now so rare and brief,
inspection is not easy' (Beckett, 1995, 184). The chronology of composition
suggests that the media of film or television informed the focus on looking,
observing and tracking the bodies trapped within the closed spaces of the prose
texts of the 1960s: *All Strange Away* was begun in August 1964, just weeks after
Beckett had returned from filming *Film* in New York (Pilling, 2006, 166). In
Beckett's plays for the television medium, which take place in closed (studio)
spaces, including *Eh Joe* from 1965, the camera or indeed the whole apparatus
of the medium is part of a technology of interrogation or surveillance. Beckett
draws on each medium to implicate the reader or the viewer in the controlling
mechanisms of the work, and also translates these modes of presentation and
perception across media. A selection of the closed space prose texts is discussed
in what follows, with a focus on repeated attempts to visually capture a figure in
a cramped cell in *All Strange Away*, and the sense of an exhausted biosphere in
Imagination Dead Imagine and *The Lost Ones*.[38]

The location of *All Strange Away* initially appears to be static, a hermetic box
with barely room for a male figure, but that figure is shown in a continual
permutation of different positions: 'sitting, standing, walking, kneeling, crawling, lying, creeping, in the dark and in the light, try all' (Beckett, 1995, 169).
The narrative voice is speculative and hypothetical, trying out different config-
urations – 'take off his coat, no, naked, all right, leave it for the moment' (170) –
or actions, such as lighting matches, or sticking black paper to the wall to try to
dim the relentless glare of the light (in vain), or erasing what has just been
imagined: 'No candle, no matches, no need, never were' (170). While the space
is cramped, time is expanded as the text progresses: 'years of time on earth'
(170), 'lifetime of unseeing glaring, eyes jammed open, one lightning wince
per minute on earth, try that' (170). But the narrator is also tracking down the
figure, like a trapped animal: 'Tighten it round him, three foot square, five high'
(170). The text then conjures women's bodies projected onto the wall, one in
particular called Emma. The gaze here becomes complex and ambiguous, as the

---

[38] Beckett worked on many variations or versions of the closed space motif during this time. *All
Strange Away* is linked to the four short prose fragments named the 'Faux départs', three of
which are in French and the final one in English, which begin to sketch out a figure in a cramped
space (Beckett, 1995, 271–3). The Fizzle 'Closed Place' (Beckett, 1995, 236–7) is related to the
composition of *The Lost Ones* in its evocation of an arena with 'Room for Millions. Wandering
and still' (199), surrounded by a track and a ditch, extending vertically 'high above the level of
the arena' (199).

erotic images of Emma —'imagine him kissing, caressing, licking, sucking, fucking and buggering all this stuff' (171) – are imagined or viewed by the figure, but also by the narrator and indeed by the reader. The position of the narrator in relation to the figure is also ambiguous, as the figure is murmuring and imagining – is he in fact the narrator, imagining or failing to imagine himself as figment: 'eyes glaring, murmuring, He's not here, no sound' (171)?

The text then performs a sexuated *volte face*. The narrator reminds us that the sex has not yet been 'seen' (172) and therefore defined, and so the figure may be female, and the projections on the wall of a male, Emmo. Yet, though the positions are mirrored, they are also stereotypically gendered, as, while the male figure is the agent of the sexual activity in the first part, Emma's fantasies are passive: 'crouching down and back she turns murmuring, Fancy her being all kissed, licked, sucked, fucked and so on by that' (172). Graham Fraser notes the repeated references to 'Fancy', and the text's obsession with permutation, often a characteristic of pornographic writing.[39] He links 'this obsessive environment of pornographic Fancy [where] the human figures are treated primarily as objects for manipulation rather than as sites of erotic possibility' (1995, 521), to Samuel Taylor Coleridge's distinction between Fancy, especially the debased or passive form of Fancy which simply collates images, and the active Imagination which transforms them.[40]

Fraser draws on Annette Kuhn's argument that the pornographic image addresses the spectator 'as desiring – desiring specifically to penetrate this "mystery" [of the woman's sex], to come to terms with it, to know it' and, in particular, it assumes that 'knowledge is to be secured through looking' (Kuhn, 1985, 40). The pornographic gaze objectifies and dissects: the narrative point of view moves like a camera over Emma's face and neck 'and thence on down to other meat [. . .] when suddenly and when least expected all this prying pointless and enough for the moment' (Beckett, 1995, 178). Indeed Fraser points out that the narrative is not only concerned with the body (male or female) in the space, but with inspecting, dissecting and measuring the space itself, defined first of all as a cube and then as a rotunda: 'The pornographic imagination in Beckett's text is equally if not more interested in the rotunda itself and the composition of the figure within it' (Fraser, 1995, 526).

---

[39] Scholars including Fraser have also traced Beckett's references to the Marquis de Sade in this text as well as in *How It Is*. See, for example, Caselli (2005), Fraser (1995, 2009), Rabaté (2016, 2020) and Weller (2009).

[40] In *Biographia Literaria*, Coleridge distinguishes between primary Imagination, a vital act of creation, and secondary Imagination 'identical with the primary in the kind of its agency and differing only in degree' (2014, 205), and Fancy, which is neither vital nor creative, but passively associates already existing images without transforming them. In Chapter IX, Coleridge mocks a writer such as George Fox, who he claims mistakes 'the tumultuous sensations of his nerves and the co-existing spectres of his fancy' for truth (105).

However, the properties of the space, like the body within it, keep permutating so no stable view can be gained despite the frequent assurance 'All that most clear' (178). Indeed the analogy of the gaze with a technological instrument such as a camera is explicitly suggested through exact timings: 'Leave for the moment as seen from outset and never doubted, slow on and off thirty seconds to glare and black any length through slow lightening and darkening greys' (179). Looking here is linked not only to the objectifying pornographic gaze, but also to the operation of the visual technology of the camera, a notion developed further in Beckett's abandoned prose text 'Long Observation of the Ray',[41] which uses a mathematical system of generation and equates the eye with the lens and shutter of a camera (see Connor, 1992). The attempt to capture the body (a term used in the context of visual imaging and hunting) also evokes anthropocentric experiments on other animals, observing their behaviour including their sexual behaviour in regulated environments. However, the narrative point of view is extremely unstable, and, after the eyelids of Emma open 'like hell gaping [. . .] and the black eye appears' (177), the narrative takes a haptic turn focusing on Emma squeezing a small rubber ball (echoes of the black ball Krapp gives to the white dog outside the nursing home where his mother was dying, or the 'old muckball' of the earth encapsulated in his lover's eyes) 'without all this poking and prying about for cracks holes and appendages' (178). The second half of the text includes references to subjective emotional states: 'Dread then in rotunda now with longing and sweet relief' (179), being 'vented as only humans can' (180), though these are expressed in the conventional terms of religion or of the Romantic tradition, which, like the references to Fancy, only emphasise the atrophied nature of concepts of 'love', 'eroticism' or 'imagination', even as the echoes of that tradition continue to faintly resonate: 'all so weak and faint no more than faint tremors of a leaf indoors on earth in winter to survive till spring' (180). What we define as human through inherited repositories of images, texts, knowledges and so on seems to fade into a post-human dusk.

Nevertheless, as James Little has argued in relation to *All Strange Away* and *Imagination Dead Imagine*, Beckett's interrogation of the 'human', explicitly mentioned in his essay on the Van Veldes,[42] never actually evacuates the human (Little, 2020, 168). Rather, in 'La peinture des Van Velde ou le monde et le pantalon', Beckett refuses any sentimental or universalised invocation of the human which perpetuates the myth that humans 'naturally' behave in a humanitarian way: 'One needs the pestilence, Lisbon and a major religious butchery for people to think of loving one another' (translation in Rabaté, 2016, 19). Beckett's writing rather demonstrates that, at the core of human subjectivity

---

[41] UoR Beckett Collection, MS 2909.   [42] Published in *Disjecta* (Beckett, 1983, 118–32).

and agency, through inherited patterns of language, representation or action, lies a tendency towards indifference, cruelty or dehumanised objectification. The incorporation of such strategies into the narration, visualisation or staging of human bodies across different media incorporates the reader/viewer/listener as witness to, indeed consumer of, such technologised scenes of subjection. Yet the shifts in point of view, as in the later sections of *All Strange Away* (or at the end of *Catastrophe*), also lead the reader/viewer to imagine the experience of the subjected or incarcerated. As John Pilling argues, 'the imagination is finding it difficult to sustain its scientific dispassionateness, and is becoming involuntarily embroiled in the lives of the figures it has summoned up' (Knowlson and Pilling, 1979, 148).

The juxtaposition of incarceration, a technologised mode of observation or generation with the traces of affective investment in the subjectivity of the body figured in the text, recurs in the short text 'Bing' / 'Ping'. 'Ping' is part of this group of texts which return again and again to the concept of figuring a body in a defined space – 'Light heat white planes shining white bare white body fixed ping fixed elsewhere' – and where mathematical or geometrical attempts to 'fix' the body in space become so excessive and repeated that any image or meaning is impossible to grasp. Although the narrative invokes traces of a human longing – 'long lashes imploring' (Beckett, 1995, 195) – the repetition of phrases increases the sense of a non-human mechanised narrative engine where 'ping' may be the name of the body or a word that deliberately resists meaning, the sound of a mechanism, for example, or, as Alys Moody suggests, 'the presence of the mechanical as an agent within the text' whose 'sporadic eruptions toggle both figure and room between various fixed states [. . .] producing the traces of what we might consider the human (speech; meaning; the animated body) as a function of its mechanised control' (2017, 94).

Yet, as Adam Piette argues in relation to the mechanisms of the narrative in *Ill Seen Ill Said*, in 'Ping' also the attempt to break down any affective response to the figure into 'pseudo-scientific' blocks, nevertheless 'displays affective symptoms at every move' (2011, 9), giving 'the lie to its own decreative drive' (17). However much the closed space texts attempt to define or capture their objects of observation in a narrative framework which 'de-centres' the human, they in fact evoke with at times uncanny tenderness the ephemerality and vulnerability of human existence. As well as performing techniques of observation on its figments, the narratives of the closed space texts therefore conjure the possibility of what Greg Garrard terms the 'kinship in mutual vulnerability' (2012b, 394) which connects humans to other living creatures on the planet, subject to environmental forces or agents beyond their control.

While these prose texts vividly evoke the spatial confinement of their human inhabitants, the continual textual deconstruction of what has been posited also prevents the establishment of any stable world to be inhabited or imagined 'whole' by the reader. Rather, the works continually operate against, while framing, the persistent objectifying mechanisms or 'syntaxes' of their construction and perception.[43] The increasing instability of the system operates at the level of both the imagined world and its textual generation. Indeed the entropic aspects of ecosystems, which may remain stable for some time and then ultimately decline, are also incorporated into Beckett's closed space texts.[44] Unlike the room or even rotunda-like space of *All Strange Away*, whose architectural references are to the Pantheon or ancient beehive tombs (Beckett, 1995, 176) inhabited by a single trapped human specimen, the spaces of *Imagination Dead Imagine* and *The Lost Ones* explicitly invoke biospheres or ecosystems with strictly regulated climates. If the narrative voice of *All Strange Away* continually revises its projected images and poses and its point of view, the narratives of *Imagination Dead Imagine* and *The Lost Ones* can imagine only exhausted, entropic worlds.[45]

The text of *Imagination Dead Imagine* expresses the need to conjure a body or bodies in a small white rotunda as the work of the not quite extinct imagination. The two bodies and their rotunda-universe are subjected to climatic forces and spatial/corporeal conditions that would be unsustainable in a 'real life' context:

> The light goes down, all grows dark together, ground, wall, vault, bodies, say twenty seconds, the light goes out, all vanishes. At the same time the temperature goes down, to reach its minimum, say freezing-point, at the instant that the black is reached, which may seem strange. (Beckett, 1995, 182–3)

The text begins by erasing the familiar earth world: 'Islands, azure, verdure, one glimpse, and vanished, endlessly, omit' (182). The bodies seem to have been generated according to an abstract pattern or set of regulations recalling the

---

[43] For this reason I see Beckett as deploying various intermedial systems of presentation and perception in these texts, even though as Little (2020) and Germoni (2007) have demonstrated, clear theatrical mechanisms are in play.

[44] Tansley argued that those ecosystems which had achieved a high level of integration and equilibrium at their peak or climax would last the longest, but that 'in others there are elements whose slow change will ultimately bring about the disintegration of the system' (1935, 301). Beckett's interest in entropy is well documented; see, for example Kurman (1975) and Jones (2008).

[45] 'For to End Yet Again' and *Lessness* are not discussed in detail here as they are set in open spaces. Nevertheless they both evoke a sense of the human species at its end, in a world turned to debris and dust.

Descartian philosophic principle of deducing models of reality by virtual paradigms, not through phenomenal observation (see Judovitz, 2001). The text refers to the fact that, because they are cramped and intertwined, 'inspection is not easy' (Beckett, 1995, 184). The positions of the two bodies are described in a similarly detached way to the figure in *All Strange Away* – 'bent in three, the arse against the wall at A, the knees against the wall between B and C' (184) and so on – and are difficult for the reader to imagine or visualise as in the earlier text.[46] This is a sterile imagination whose capacity for bringing forth a world is reduced to the barest remains of the human. The bodies are gendered as 'woman' (184) and her male partner, though any specific gender markings or differences between the bodies are absent.

The references here are to an imagination at its own limits, 'imagination dead imagine'. Yet the text gives life to this cell of human being, so that the 'eye of prey' (185) can consume it, and then erases it in another of Beckett's stories which perform their own end and rehearse ending itself:

> No, life ends, and no, there is nothing elsewhere, and no question now of ever finding again that white speck lost in whiteness, to see if they still lie in the stress of that storm, or of a worse storm, or in the black dark for good, or the great whiteness unchanging, and if not what they are doing. (185)

Ironically, the ending confirms the continuing hunger of the 'eye of prey' to imagine what they are doing, and therefore confirms that imagination is not dead yet. Indeed, Beckett returned to the concept of imagining and detailing a dying biosphere in *The Lost Ones*.

The Lost Ones: Imagining the End of the Human

The Lost Ones narrates even more overtly a microcosm of the human species. Several genetic traces reach back to 'Espace souterrain'. For instance, *The Lost Ones* evokes, as in the earlier fragment, an 'abode where lost bodies roam each searching for its lost one' (Beckett, 1995, 202). While the spatial boundaries of the mud through which bodies crawl in *How It Is* remain undefined, the abode the lost ones inhabit is visualised as a cylinder, apparently hermetic, though the inhabitants keep searching for a 'way out'. The cylinder consists of a crowded central arena 'One body per square metre or two hundred bodies in all round numbers' (204), where those who are still searching 'with unceasing eyes' (212) roam or come to rest against the walls. Rather than holes in the ground, however, into which the bodies disappear in 'Espace souterrain', the upper

---

[46] Nevertheless, Beckett made continual drawings of the spatial arrangement of the confined body in the draft versions of *All Strange Away* as enclosed in a letter to Barbara Bray on 22 September 1964 (Beckett, 2014, 628). See Little (2020, chapter 8).

half of the cylinder in *The Lost Ones* is pitted with niches, some linked by tunnels, so that some of the 'little people' (205) of the abode who choose to be 'climbers' rather than 'searchers' make use of a series of ladders to climb up to them. The narrator imagines 'a perfect mental picture of the entire system' (204). However, such a precise visual image would be an abstraction, as the environment of the cylinder is in continual fluctuation, not just the ceaseless movement of at least some of the inhabitants, but also its 'climate' (219). This hermetic ecosystem exists in a continually oscillating rhythm of temperature between hot and cold, and a dim, omnipresent, yellow light, sometimes 'agleam' and sometimes still (202). The bodies in the abode are of the human species only, though the narrator invokes comparisons with 'insects' (214) and 'butterflies' (207).

Human bodies are therefore placed under an ethnographic gaze in this text, as if they were a colony of ants, and the observer is imagined as a 'thinking being coldly intent on all these data and evidences' (214). Porter Abbott has compared *The Lost Ones* to the nineteenth-century trope of the exploratory adventure, which 'was historically front-loaded with a colonial fascination for racial and ethnic exotics, but, coming after *The Origin of Species* (1859), it combined this fascination with an attitude of anthropological interest' (Abbott, 2002, 1). Indeed the tone of the narrator who, with apparent scientific detachment, notes the desiccating impact of the climate on the mucous membranes of the bodies and that of the light on the increasingly reddened and perished eyes of the searchers (Beckett, 1995, 214), is disturbing to read. The history of the anthropocentric drive towards scientific observation as a technique of knowledge is satirised and turned on its head as it is the human species whose habitat and behaviours are objectified, described, measured and named only in their namelessness: 'The quidam then quits his post in search of a free ladder or to join the nearest or shortest queue' (205).[47]

And yet this detached, all-knowing narrator also undoes their own knowledge. As they describe the satisfaction of someone with 'long experience and detailed knowledge' achieving a 'perfect mental picture' of the aforementioned scene, they admit that 'it is doubtful that such a one exists' (204). A hypothetical note is introduced – 'this notion [. . .] if it is maintained' (205) – and returns as the last words of the text: 'if this notion is maintained' (223). The narrator also introduces what cannot be known by the searchers, the narrator or the reader: 'In the cylinder alone are certitudes to be found and without nothing but mystery' (216). Yet the description of the cylinder also becomes increasingly speculative

---

[47] An exception to this lack of individuation is the specific mention of the 'vanquished' woman who orients the searchers as 'She is the north' (221).

when, after the detailed spatial descriptions of the first few pages, the narrative begins to imagine 'a vast space of time impossible to measure' (213) and, in particular, the gradual entropic decline of the inhabitants to the moment when 'this last of all if a man [. . .] slowly draws himself up and sometime later opens his burnt eyes' (223). The narrative announces itself as fiction and therefore, as in so many of Beckett's works, both evokes and unravels the relationship of creator and creature. Yet the reader is implicated in this perceptual and conceptual relation to the 'little people of searchers' (223), even when no single one, with the exception of the vanquished woman occupying the position of the north, or the last man, is singled out, and though they are seen entirely from an exterior perspective. Beckett provides enough connections with the references to the cylinder and the 'orb' of the eyes for us to see in this abode a microcosm of what our species might look like from the point of view of an external 'intelligence' (212) or 'thinking being' (214). In the climate emergency of the twenty-first century this image of a round abode which is becoming uninhabitable is profoundly evocative.

Moreover, the resonance of 'if a man' with Primo Levi's *If This Is a Man* underlines the subtext not only of ethnography, but also of the camps of the Second World War, where a mechanical, dehumanising and exterminating ideology was perpetrated on some sectors of the human species by another. Several scholars have thought through the complex and intersecting issues of testimony, language and subjectivity raised by Beckett's overt reference to Levi, including the issues of who can testify on behalf of those who did not survive, named the drowned or the 'musulmen' in Levi, which seem to correspond to the 'vanquished' in *The Lost Ones*.[48] I am interested here in how Beckett's closed space narration initially traps the reader into occupying the position of an apparently detached and scientific – even dehumanising – observer, and yet, as the narrative progresses, the despair and exhaustion of the 'little people' seeps into it, and the affective power of this perspective on the finitude of human existence begins to operate as the reader views the human species and its habitation from a perspective which places its entire history on this small planet in eons of time from the 'unthinkable first day' (212) to 'this last of all', when the abode will simply be a burnt shell.

In the later prose and audiovisual media, the act of observation is almost always interrogated in connection to the relations of power and control between seer and seen, including anthropological or scientific perspectives, that of an indifferent creator impassively viewing the entropy of its imagined world, or even a mechanical function. Yet the omniscience and authority of the creator

---

[48] See, for example, Anderton (2016), Katz (2009), Jones (2011) and Weber-Caflisch (1994).

figure or function within the text, or indeed that of the reader/observer, is also undermined. Several scholars have noted the contradictions within the narrative evocation of texts such as *All Strange Away* or *The Lost Ones* which prevent the reader's establishment of any total mental picture of these spaces and their inhabitants. Michelle Rada argues that:

> Even though *The Lost Ones* incessantly measures and describes the cylinder as an enclosed whole, the text consistently refuses any form of closure [. . .] The text's narrative machinery is laid bare and its mastery undermined, perhaps proposing a model for speaking and reading that interrupts totality rather than enforcing it, or that bores holes rather than sealing, disavowing, or collapsing them. (Rada, 2018, 37)

As Connor notes, the imaginative faculty in much of the late work is exhausted, the mechanisms worn out and barely functioning. And yet it is perhaps these exhausted worlds that both testify to and refuse the Cartesian thinking that would posit a world as *res* to be possessed by (some) humans. Timothy Morton wonders if 'the approach to nature as *res* entail[s] thinking of it as a vivisectable being to whom we can do infinite sadistic violence as "possessors and masters of nature"', and considers that 'the only firm ethical option in the current catastrophe [. . .] is admitting to the ecologically catastrophic in all its meaningless contingency' (Morton 2007, 204). Morton emphasises that human culture is also a part of the planet's ecological history, not only in the damaging and unequal impact of the Anthropocene, but also in producing potential resources that might offer alternative models of being and inhabiting the earth, or indeed, in helping us to imagine a world that may no longer be habitable for humans or other species. Morton's concept of dark ecology posits the world as profoundly unhomely and acknowledges the affective impact of such an uncanny insight. He defines dark ecology as 'saturated with unrequited longing' (2007, 186, and Morton, 2016).

The next section explores Beckett's teleplays, where, I argue, television is not exploited solely as a technology of observation, but becomes a medium of poetic longing and invocation: the Yeatsian poem 'The Tower' is visualised faintly as the face of a woman in *. . . but the clouds . . .*, and Schubert's lied in *Nacht und Träume* produces religiously inflected dreamscapes in which the dreamer is provisionally comforted by hands mopping his brow or quenching his thirst. The images in these television plays are blurred, difficult to see or only occasionally glimpsed, and the visual is continually in dialogue with poetry or music which destabilises its authority. Indeed, the teleplays exploit the technologically mediated gaze of the television to intensify the uncanny effects of these ghosts of the Romantic tradition.

4 Televisual Systems and Romantic Ghosts of the Anthropocene

The early 1960s was a time of experimentation across different media for Beckett, where the worlds evoked in each work became ever more closely modelled on the features, technologies and modes of reception of the medium in which it was created. For example, having written the radio play *All That Fall* in 1957, which vividly evokes the human, animal and floral life of the environs of Dublin in the 1930s (although its production depended on innovative technologies to edit and denaturalise the sound world it created), Beckett's later radio drama focuses increasingly on the medium itself, its aural components and its conditions of production and broadcast reception.[49] *Rough for Radio II* (1961) features an interrogation session which is recording the utterances of the bound Fox, and *Words and Music* (1961) presents an elderly feudal lord, Croak, in a Yeatsian tower with his two retainers or 'comforts' (Beckett, 1986, 287), the eponymous and anthropomorphised Words and Music. In *Cascando*, also written in 1961, the sonic world of the play is operated by an Opener who opens and closes, streams singly or mixes the two channels of Voice and Music. Although Voice visualises the story of Woburn drifting far out to sea in another perlocutionary tale of ending, Opener is a function, not an aurally embodied character, and apart from Voice's narrative, no spatial environment is evoked, closed or otherwise, not even the interior of Opener's head (299). Rather, the medium of the radio and its materials, whether human voice, sound or music, function as a kind of non-anthropocentric circuit in Joe Milutis' terms, which includes the listener: 'The body becomes a radio system [. . .] rather than a radio set. It is transmitter, receiver, and director in one. The lines between production and consumption are broken down in this system' (1996, 71).

Beckett abandoned radio as a mode of composition after *Cascando*, though not its acousmatic qualities (see Morin, 2014) or its focus on incorporating the listener into a mediated system or circuit, both of which he translated into his work in other media. In theatre, Beckett finished *Happy Days* in January 1961 and the German premiere of his next stage play, *Spiel* (*Play*), was held in Ulm in June 1963. As discussed in Section 2, *Play* eliminates any referential location: it is set in darkness where the three 'characters' are visible only as heads emerging from funereal urns trapped in a narrow circuit of moving light and interrupted speech. The text is spoken at speed and repeated in its entirety with even a third cycle begun, so that, although the middle-class world of the narrative is glimpsed in fragments, in performance the focus is on what Ruby Cohn has described as the 'theaterreality' of what is happening in front of the audience

---

[49] See Zilliacus (1976), Bignell (2009) and Laws (2017) for more detail on the BBC production.

(1980, 28). Although, on one level, the darkness is open to different interpretations so that its dimensions are unclear – whether a small crypt, a post-human
limbo where time has turned into undefined space, or an interior mind space – it
is also the circumscribed space of the theatre stage, illuminated by that most
theatrical of stage lighting, a spotlight. The play draws attention to the stage
itself and to its technologies, yet references to judgement and pity evoke the
Christian cosmology and non-anthropocentric temporality of Purgatory and the
hope of salvation (articulated here as simply silence and darkness), as in *How It
Is*, though the subordination of the three heads to a repetition that seems to have
been going on since time immemorial reduces such references to empty phrases.
The continually shifting temporal and spatial planes due to the motion of the
Light and the speed of the heads' speech prevent any stable visual or aural
capture of the stage image. Like so much of Beckett's later drama across
different media, the audience members are implicated as witnesses, interroga-
tors and part of the theatrical system which traps the heads in their urns and
subjects them to the Light's interrogation. As David Pattie has argued, 'in the
theatre, the coercive system exists outside of the text – in the mechanisms of the
theatre itself', but, drawing on Gilles Deleuze's theories of negative imma-
nence, he points out that 'the coercer and the coerced are subject to the apparent
entropy of the Beckettian universe' (2018, 232). Indeed, the Light in *Play* is also
caught up in the mechanisms of repetition, wavering and fading in the course of
the second repetition.

Much of Beckett's work in the 1960s, therefore, whatever the medium,
excludes the recognisable exterior world in order to focus on self-consciously
constructed and technologically mediated environments which position their
human subjects in increasingly delimited spaces subject to laws, regulations and
technologies that both generate and constrain the creation of the fictional world.
As mentioned in the previous section, a new medium also opened up at this
time, as Beckett was invited to write the script for a film in a series commis-
sioned by Barney Rosset in the early 1960s. In 1963, Beckett sent an outline of
Film to Grove Press, and filming took place in the summer of 1964 in New York
(Knowlson, 1996, 520–5).[50] After the experience of filming *Film*, Beckett
turned to television and wrote *Eh Joe* in 1965. As examined in what follows,
Beckett's work for the small screen intensifies the preoccupation with scrutin-
ising a human body or face as mediated by the camera, but in fact this looking
reveals very little about the figures on the screen or the details of their environment. Indeed, as in the closed space prose, the human figure is increasingly
imaged as one element in the overall compositional system that constructs an

---

[50] See also Schneider (1995), where he discusses directing *Film*.

interior room space, but also destabilises it while drawing attention to the mechanisms of its construction. So, although some of these plays seem at first to be set in a box, they increasingly fracture and dislocate both spatial and temporal co-ordinates, subverting the search for knowledge or enlightenment through looking.

The teleplays therefore continue a concern with the subjection of human figures to systems of constraint in order to facilitate external observation while foregrounding the mediating conditions of camera and sound recording and broadcast, where, unlike the theatre, the bodies of the actors are transformed into shadows (though Beckett's late theatre attempts to simulate this ghostliness through lighting, costume, make-up and so on).[51] Beckett exploits this ghostliness and lack of flesh to focus on increasingly abstracted visual textures and patterns, which, as several scholars have shown, recall other visual media, especially painting.[52] Some of them also include music, so that listening competes with looking as the dominant mode of perception and interpretation. Indeed, as Graley Herren has demonstrated, the teleplays are saturated with fragments and ghosts of human conceptual and artistic production:

> many of them premodern, and ranging across the cultural spectrum, from philosophy to psychology, to classical music and painting, through poetry and silent films to sculpture and dance. [. . .] The teleplays simultaneously engage and estrange tradition, invoking artistic predecessors only to resist, refute, and revise them. (Herren, 2007, 5)

This section focuses mainly on Beckett's teleplays as televisual ecosystems where the human figure is one element in the entire composition, and where the operation of that system increasingly deconstructs the stability or wholeness of the visual space that it presents, defamiliarising the viewer's usual perceptual frameworks and construction of space and time. The construction of the teleplays from the traces and fragments of other texts also questions our relationship

---

[51] Jennifer Fay has discussed the long-standing attribution of the uncanny to the cinema screen, quoting Maxim Gorky on viewing the Lumière films exhibited in 1896:

> Yesterday I was in the Kingdom of Shadows . . . Everything there – the earth, the trees, the people, the water and the air – is tinted in a grey monotone: in a grey sky there are grey rays of sunlight; in grey faces, grey eyes, and the leaves of the trees are grey like ashes. This is not life but the shadow of life and this is not movement but the soundless shadow of movement. (quoted in Fay, 2018, 3)

[52] See for example, Knowlson and Haynes (2003). Both Bignell (2009) and Paraskeva (2017) discuss Beckett's use of techniques associated with avant-garde cinema in the teleplays. For example, Paraskeva analyses Beckett's references to 'the early period of silent filmmaking and theory, and second wave modernism's ghost-like re-animation of silent film techniques' in . . . *but the clouds* . . . (2017, 144–5).

to a history of representations, including Romantic conceptions of subjectivity, gender and nature.

Film: In Pursuit of a Completed Visual Circuit from Exterior to Interior

Although the focus of this section is on selected teleplays, *Eh Joe* follows *Film* so closely that it is worth beginning with Beckett's one and only film. *Film* features an ageing Buster Keaton, recalling the heyday of silent film in its star, its anachronistic black-and-white aesthetic and largely silent soundtrack, and its period of 'about 1929' (Beckett, 1986, 324).[53] Significant from the perspective of ecosystems and spatial frames is the retraction of space from the margins of an exterior cityscape in the opening shots of Keaton scuttling along a wall in an area of high-rise apartments to an interior room, culminating in a confrontation between O (object) and E (eye) as split perceptual functions of a divided self, O seeking to escape perception and E as the drive or hunger towards completing the circuit of perception.[54]

Film therefore visualises different ecosystems. The first, described in the script of *Film*, is set in a '*small factory district*' and depicts '*moderate animation of workers going unhurriedly to work*' (324). The absence in these workers of any anxiety around perceiving or being perceived establishes a contrast with the solitary figure of O in flight from any 'extraneous perception' (323). However, the description of these workers foregrounds a highly systematised order of movement and groupings, focusing less on independent 'sovereign' individuals than on the pattern of interactions between them: '*All going in same direction and all in couples. No automobiles. Two bicycles ridden by men with girl passengers (on crossbar)* [...] *all contentedly in* percipere *and* percipi' (324).[55] The urban ecosystem of paired workers suggests a mechanised routine that may be linked to industrialisation – the pairs are mainly on bicycles, but the script mentions one horse-driven cab whose driver is '*standing brandishing whip*' (324). This recalls Christy's hinny from *All That Fall*, but *Film*'s 'nag' seems especially vulnerable to human violence as the sole representative of the more than human species in this man-made industrialised cityscape. Through the scenes of O attempting to escape the perception of his fellow animal creatures (who he treats with care and tenderness) as well as divine surveillance

---

[53] See Bignell (2009, 133–8) and Paraskeva (2017, 37–71).

[54] In the transcription of pre-production published in Gontarski (1985, 187–92), Beckett emphasised the contrast he wanted between 'the maximum of exposed exterior, or man completely exposed, and then another, the maximum of protected interior, enclosed, seclusion' (190).

[55] Ross Lipman's 2016 kino-essay *Not Film* has restored this section of *Film*, notoriously rendered unusable in the final version because of overexposure.

(he violently rips up the god image), *Film* dramatises a sceptical view of a progressive, futurist utopia built on industrialised production which leads not only to regularised efficient movement, but also to the human subjection of other creatures like the nag, and indeed to an increasingly mediated vision where the operation of visual perception itself through the camera is conceptualised as 'pursuit' (323).

Once the camera shifts from the initial street scene to focus on O, viewers become aware of the insistent presence of the camera which tracks O. E is, on one hand, anthropomorphised in terms of the camera's positioning just behind O as if E were a person following O, and yet the fact that E is manifested as the eye of the camera confronting other human and non-human creatures (the monkey, for example) creates the uncanny sense of a kino-eye, a perceptual function which has fused with a technological/prosthetic device.[56] The perception of O, by contrast, is revealed as partial and degraded because of his eye patch, a convention that enables viewers to distinguish between what O sees and what E as camera sees (outside O's subjective point of view). Only at the end, when all other eyes have been eliminated, is E completely anthropomorphised into an inscrutable double of O, complete with eye patch.

In order to escape being perceived by others, O retreats into a '*small barely furnished room*' (326) in a block of flats. As soon as he enters, he closes and locks the door and carefully creeps along the walls until he gets to the window, where he lowers the tattered blind. The room is now (apparently) a secure, enclosed space. Nevertheless, this room contains in miniature a medieval/ Elizabethan 'chain of being' as 'an ordered universe arranged in a fixed system of hierarchies' (Tillyard, 1943, 5–6), except that the hierarchies that placed man above the rest of creation seem to have been disrupted: from the inanimate chair to the fish, cat, dog, human and divine in the pinned image on the wall behind the chair, all are reduced to staring eyes, each of which O tries to eject, evade or destroy. Just when he thinks he has succeeded, and he is about to relax and slip out of consciousness into sleep, E exceeds the angle of immunity it has observed until now,[57] and confronts O with the apparition of his own self-perception and double, illustrating *Film*'s thesis that 'All extraneous perception suppressed, animal, human, divine, self-perception maintains in being' (323). No matter

---

[56] Film director Dziga Vertov coined the term 'kino-eye' to describe an approach to cinematography that did not seek to imitate human visual perception, but assembled fragments and perspectives that celebrated the fusion of technology and the body, as in his film *Man with a Movie Camera* (1929).

[57] According to Jonathan Bignell, 'The 45 degree rule whereby Keaton can be safe from the camera's perception if the camera remains behind him at less than this angle [...] appears to allude to the impossibility of seeing oneself in a mirror if positioned beyond 45 degrees to one side' (2009, 194).

how many times O locks the door, this closed space, like so many of Beckett's transmedial closed spaces of the 1960s, fails to be impregnable. Somehow the eye of the camera and of the viewer can cross the boundaries of this supposedly hermetic space.

Film therefore focuses at least partially on an obsession with completed self-perception in a quest to recover the sense of an integrated self. However, this quest is frustrated by the split between O and E, O's resistance to being perceived and the predatory nature of E as camera, entangling the viewers also in its insistent gaze. But the viewer's gaze has also been split: as Crary has argued, the paradigm of vision where the observer views a stable external world or object is fractured by the operation of the camera and the mediated series of eyes in *Film*, including the close-up of the eyelid at the opening. Indeed, the referential function of the room space also at times dissolves into a focus on the texture and tatters of disintegrating plaster, net curtains or blind, creating some haunting, almost abstract images. While articulating the anxiety, fragmentation and loss experienced by the human subject who is not integrated into the industrial urban machine, *Film* also prefigures the impact of technology and mediation not only on human motion, but also on the fundamental structures of subjectivity and perception. At the same time, the insistent though marginal presence of various animals in *Film* recognises the impact of industrialised modernity not only on human subjects, but also on the more than human world. The anachronistic time frame and black-and-white 'poor' aesthetic increase the 'unreal' quality of the visual world of the film, emphasising that the work itself is a filmic artefact. As ever, Beckett reflects on his own processes of production and that of the creative and technical team as well as that of the viewer who is positioned by the film as also participating in the scopic drive which pursues and preys on its object, and which, in the end, turns on itself. In the subsequent television plays, the protagonists remain within interior rooms or closed spaces, and yet, like O's room in *Film*, these closed spaces cannot exclude external observation. While retaining the visual representation of an interior scene, these teleplays increasingly incorporate the viewer into the systems that constitute them, so that any 'objective' vision of space or figure is also destabilised.

Eh Joe: Dislocating Audio and Visual Circuits

Unlike O in *Film*, Joe in Beckett's first television play is only ever seen in an interior room. However, Joe also checks all the doors and windows to ensure no external intruder can enter. He looks under the bed to make sure no one is hiding there. The establishing shot of the room indicates that this is a domestic interior, but, as Jonathan Bignell argues, this and other interior spaces in Beckett's teleplays 'are quite clearly constructed sets rather than locations' (2009, 144).

In the BBC version, and to an even greater extent in the German Süddeutscher Rundfunk (SDR) *He, Joe*, the location is evidently a television studio, with bare walls and windows/doors emphasising the abstracted visual geometry of the set. After the initial inspection of the space, there is almost no action, except that of the camera which focuses in increasing close-up on Joe's face, while an acousmatic female voice-over accuses Joe of a series of abandonments and of morbid self-pity: 'Sitting there in your foul old wrapper' (Beckett, 1986, 364). However, the interrelationship between the female Voice and Joe is never clarified. Is she an exteriorisation of Joe's guilty conscience, a memory or a ghostly visitation? Does the screen represent the interior space of Joe's mind which he seeks to render impervious by committing 'mental thuggee' (363) on the voices of departed family and lovers that invade his head, or that of some other being or function? Voice's verbal attacks are co-ordinated with the movements of the camera focusing more and more intensely on Joe's face, so that the whole audiovisual system of the teleplay seems to perform an interrogation of or judgement upon Joe and his life, intensified through religious references to 'your Lord' and the parable in the Gospel of Luke, 'Thou fool thy soul' (364). As in almost all of Beckett's closed space works, the apparently hermetic interior somehow accommodates the intrusion of the perceiving other, while that position is multiple and unstable: at once self or other, Joe, the Voice, the camera and the viewer.

The external world re-emerges in the narrative of the Voice, with scenes of the embodied persona of the Voice as Joe's lover watching ducks in Dublin's St Stephen's Green on summer evenings, and later the various attempts of another of Joe's lovers, the green one, to commit suicide by drowning herself. The portrayal of the green one contrasts with the self-absorbed obsession of both Joe and the Voice who are locked in a struggle within the enclosed space of the room / Joe's head / the television set. The green one is shown in relation to the moon (*'Always pale'*) and the tide; indeed at times she becomes indistinguishable from them: 'Clawing at the shingle now ... [...] Imagine the *eyes* ... Spirit light' (366). *Eh Joe* therefore juxtaposes a Romanticised depiction of the green one in the open spaces of the moonlit shore, contrasted with the vindictive tone of Voice and its quality of 'flint glass'(363),[58] and Joe's guilt-ridden, self-absorbed interior mind space. This association of the female with a Romantic anthropomorphic tradition will recur in later teleplays, including *Ghost Trio* and *... but the clouds ...* .

However, the ending further destabilises perceptual and subject positions as Voice instructs Joe to imagine himself in the place of the girl 'Taking Joe with her' (366) as an act of erasure of the world of the teleplay and the hellish mind

---

[58] See McTighe (2013) on the haptic qualities of the voice in *Eh Joe* and throughout Beckett's work.

space it evokes: '*Voice and image out. End.*' (367). The actual teleplay in both the BBC and SDR versions does not end with that blackout, but with the camera drawing back to focus on Joe's face, on which a smile emerges, as perhaps he has managed to silence Voice, at least for the night. The unfolding of the teleplay, while apparently devoid of action, is suffused with violence – Joe's attempts to suppress Voice, apparently gaining ground as the Voice fades to an aggressive whisper, Voice's accusatory assaults on Joe, and, in Voice's narrative, the Gillette razor blade which the green one tries to use in order to commit suicide, but which creates only a scratch before she finally swallows a bottle of pills. The close of the play figures a struggle to end on all the narrative, visual and aural channels of the teleplay. The movement of the camera closing in on Joe's face also implicates the viewer in its interrogation of Joe, miming an attempt to extract knowledge or evidence. However, Joe's expression remains inscrutable.[59] Although the tension in MacGowran's BBC performance, for example, registers anxiety in the large eyes and creased face, we cannot be sure how to read this: does it express guilt, his efforts to strangle the voice, or pain at the memory of the dead girl evoked by Voice? The viewer is thereby placed in a dilemma. With what function of the apparatus do we identify? Are we complicit with the interrogatory Voice accusing Joe, do we sympathise with Joe as victim of the voice, however guilty he might be, or rather with the girl who committed suicide for which Voice seems to hold Joe to account? The drama is in the operation of the televisual system itself and how it positions the viewer in its network or circuit of Joe, Voice and camera. As Bignell argues, the teleplays subvert the relationship between the subject who looks (including the viewer) and the object looked at, so that, although they are 'structured as observation', because 'the perceiving subject and the object perceived remain ungrasped and lacking, these audio-visual texts deconstruct the stability of observation on which they appear to be based' (2009, 162).

Ghost Trio, ... *but the clouds* ... and *Nacht und Träume*: Audiovisual Systems for Summoning Ghosts of the Romantic Anthropocene

It would be more than ten years until Beckett's next television play was broadcast in 1977 as part of BBC's Lively Arts programme Shades, which also included ... *but the clouds* ... and a televised version of *Not I*.[60] In *Ghost*

---

[59] See Bignell (2009, 45–7) on how *Eh Joe* disrupts usual televisual conventions of witnessing and close-up.

[60] However, during this time, Beckett had been thinking about visual media in an unfinished project and manuscript in French entitled 'Film-Vidéo-Cassette projet', dated November 1972. As Mark Nixon has argued, this project described on two pages of text and two drawings anticipates *Ghost*

Trio, written in 1975, the subject is male, waiting for a female loved one who
does not arrive: the play was originally titled 'Tryst' (Gontarski, 1985, 122).
This figure F is isolated in the 'familiar chamber' and, like Joe, checks the doors
and windows, though seemingly in hope of the arrival of the woman for whom
he waits rather than from the desire to escape or repress her. However, again, the
enclosure of this room is breached. There is a female voice-over V who is not
located in the space of the room and who does not seem to be inside F's head;
rather she seems to address the viewer as the voice of the televisual medium,
instructing the viewer to 'keep that sound down' (Beckett, 1986, 408), and also
mediating between sound and vision, the viewer and the spectral figure on the
screen. She apparently controls the movements of F almost like a puppet. Indeed
several accounts mention Beckett's overt references to Kleist's *übermarionnette*
during the rehearsals of the BBC *Ghost Trio*.[61] The studio location has been
further abstracted with geometrical patterning of door, window and pallet. The
whole scenario seems to be one whose repetition has become mechanical and
programmed, emphasised by its three-part structure: pre-action, action, reac-
tion. The human figure in *Ghost Trio* is presented not as an autonomous agent,
but only in interrelationship with every element of the audiovisual broadcast
and with the overall structure and operation of the system. V invites, indeed
commands the viewer to visually inspect the system: 'Now look closer' (408).
The system has been set up to be perceptually 'consumed', so the viewer is an
integral part of its operation. Toby Zinman cites Beckett's description of
television as a 'peephole art' in her essay on *Eh Joe*, which suggests
a voyeuristic mode of looking inherent in the medium (Zinman, 1995).

However, the apparent hermeticism and mechanisms of control are undermined by the moment when F disobeys V's instructions, and also by elements
which escape or elude visual representation and control. This includes extracts
from Beethoven's Piano Trio in D, Opus 70, No. 1, *Geistertrio*, which gives the
teleplay its title, and whose visible diegetic source is a cassette player clutched
by the waiting figure.[62] The music also seems to evoke the interior, affective
state of the figure to which we otherwise have no access. This interpretation
depends on the work of the viewer-listener to connect the disjointed visual

---

Trio in its theme of waiting for someone who does not arrive, and the self-conscious use of the
medium, as the woman F1 waits in the first film, then F2 watches a video of that earlier film in
the second part, with some playing with mirrors that picks up themes of self-perception from
Film. Without much sense of any text, the focus here is on the manipulation of technology in
relation to a sense of loss and absence which renders the subject totally isolated and self-
enclosed, except for the contemplation of her own past self/selves (Nixon, 2009).
[61] See Knowlson (1986) and Tucker (2015).
[62] Knowlson points out a further ghostly reference: Beethoven was working on an opera of
Shakespeare's *Macbeth* as he was composing *Geistertrio* (1996, 621).

frames to the musical extracts, which, as Catherine Laws has demonstrated, Beckett has also selected and rearranged.[63] The system reveals its own artifice, and, as Herren notes, presents itself as constructed from a history of musical, poetic and visual artistic endeavours, and especially the legacy of Romanticism through the music of Beethoven. Indeed, as in the television play Beckett would write just a year or so after *Ghost Trio*, ... *but the clouds* ..., this Romantic legacy is linked to the construction of gender in the play.

Laws explains that Beckett tends to start on the second bar of the chosen sections, rearranges the temporal order of some extracts, and omits the second subject material until the playing of the coda (2013, 148). Since classical music tradition tends to designate the first subject material as 'male' and the second as 'female', Laws argues that Beckett's rearrangement of the Beethoven music emphasises anticipation on the part of the listening figure for the female and his eventual imaginative re-evocation of her through the playing of the coda. However, this imaginative structure (as in Joe's attempts to inhabit the last moments of the green one's expiring consciousness) also suggests the interdependence of the 'masculine' and 'feminine' roles:

> Beckett's choices exaggerate the uncertainty of the construction of (male) identity in the Beethoven, focusing instead on a transitory stage of passage towards a second (female) subject that is itself for the most part elusive: he evokes a state between self and other, or perhaps the 'Neither' of 'self and unself'. (Laws, 2013, 148)

Ghost Trio therefore 'denies us the possibility of identifying the imaginative responsibility with any individual agent' (Laws, 2013, 151), so that the one waiting and the absent one are both interrelated parts of the overall structure, including the gendered structure of self and other.

Jonathan Bignell also argues that, although several of the teleplays feature 'an apparently masculine subject [which] ambivalently and questionably constitutes itself by imagining a feminine other from which it is separated and which it desires [...] the feminine that the masculine subject imagines is not represented as a fictional fantasy' (2009, 113). Rather, 'the feminine and masculine are established in relation to each other' (114). The absent one, referred to only as 'her', is presented in relation to the figure's aural anticipation of her: 'He will now think he hears her' (Beckett, 1986, 410). Part of the Romantic legacy is the positing of the subject (usually though not exclusively male) as founded on loss and yearning, often for a 'belle dame sans merci' as in Keats' poem.[64] The

---

[63] See also Maier (2001) and (2002).

[64] See, for example, *Samuel Beckett Today / Aujourdhui* 18.1 (Van Hulle and Nixon, 2007) on Beckett and Romanticism, Tonning (2007, 180–5) and Brater (2011, 102–14). At the end of the

masculine and feminine figures (whether absent or visualised) of *Ghost Trio* and ... *but the clouds* ... can therefore be seen as founded on a binary gender imaginary whose syntax has been shaped through historical convention. Like the structure of the musical score, Beckett draws attention to the constructed-ness of the system by disrupting or destabilising some of its elements. The apparent gender binary between F who, though presented as relatively andro-gynous with long white hair and robe, is referred to as 'he' and the female for whom he waits, is complicated by the fact that the Voice is also female, so there are two contrasting representations of the feminine – one associated with a functional operation of the medium apparently exterior to the figure, contra-dicting, as Zinman has argued, the usual voyeuristic structure of male viewer and female figure viewed, and one as the Romantic inaccessible other, associ-ated with the interior structure of affectivity and longing which the action and soundscape seem to attribute to F. Moreover the figure who does appear at the end is not female but a young boy. The viewer might interpret his shake of the head to mean that, like Godot, F's awaited female visitor will not appear tonight, but the boy also doubles F, like a younger version of his self. In the BBC version, the boy appears as rather cherubic, his black oilskin 'glistening with rain' (Beckett, 1986, 413), but in the SDR version, the boy is presented in a much more spectral and uncanny way (Knowlson, 1986). As Laws argues in relation to Beckett's use of the music, rather than a binary opposition, these male and female figures seem to be part of the operation of a system, but one whose boundaries seem increasingly dissolved into fragments and shadows.

The visual boundaries of the closed interior also collapse. In Part I, sup-posedly focused on establishing 'the familiar chamber', the camera shifts from a long shot of the room, as in *Eh Joe*, to individual close-up shots of the wall or pallet revealing only rectangles of 'dust', which flicker in the analogue trans-mission. The figure is also fragmented and duplicated when his face is seen in close-up, first in a mirror (followed by a shot of his tangled hair like some abstract painting as he bows his head) in Part II, and then directly on screen in Part III when F raises his head at the end of the play. In the third part, diegetic sound is suddenly added; rain can be heard (and seen) falling and the door creaks as it opens, which seems to reflect more of F's perceptual point of view in that the viewer sees and hears what he hears, and the controlling V has fallen silent. Nevertheless, as Laws argues, the viewer-listener is never sure where

---

'Closed Space' Fizzle, the text refers to 'beldam nature' (Beckett, 1995, 237). See also Praz [1930] (1954), especially chapter 4 on 'La Belle Dame sans Merci'. Beckett read and took notes from the original Italian edition of *The Romantic Agony* in the early 1930s (Beckett, 1999, 36–8, 45–6).

subjectivity lies, as the formal structure of both audio and visual elements keeps shifting the focus back to F as a figure in a composition.

However, the author of the composition both is and isn't Beckett. As in the radio plays *Words and Music* and *Cascando*, while Beckett is the named author of *Ghost Trio*, authority is fractured and shared with the composer since the title is also an English translation of the title of the Beethoven trio, and indeed, Beckett worked very closely with the BBC and SDR creative and technical teams in order to realise the work. While acknowledging Beckett's privileged status as an author at the BBC when these teleplays were made, Bignell also examines the deconstruction of the author function in the teleplays, where 'the medium and its allusions to other media, and the author and his role [are] one node among a paradigmatic and syntagmatic complex of textual sites' (2009, 163). Herren also argues that this complex fabric of aural and visual citations (including modern art works from cubism to Rothko, for example) presents the teleplay as a stage/screen on which fragments, layers and ghosts of other works appear. Though these may be human-authored, the technical medium itself is integral to their patterns of aural and visual composition.

As Laws has suggested, these teleplays share a particular focus on the Romantic tradition, signalled by their use of Romantic composers. In addition to the longing for an inaccessible other, evoking the unrealisable ideal or sublime, or embodying the poetic muse, the Romantic conceptualisation of nature as anthropomorphic or sublime is also evoked and subverted.[65] In *Eh Joe*, the green one was associated with the Romantic figure of endless yearning, the moon. In *Ghost Trio* also, the figure's waiting evokes but also denaturalises tropes where the outer landscape reflects subjective moods of isolation or contemplation, as in the paintings of Caspar David Friedrich. In Part III, when the figure opens the window, viewers hear and see rain falling, but the sound and image are suddenly switched on and off, revealing them as effects created in the studio, emphasising that this 'nature' is constructed and technologically mediated. The very concept of nature is framed as 'already an idea, a trope or cultural construct produced by humans for their own purposes' (Lavery and Finburgh, 2015, 18). Yet, even when both flesh and nature seem to have withered away or have been replaced by a technologically programmed world, the longing for an 'other' as part of the constitution of the self persists. The teleplays suggest that that other may be art: poetry, music or painting. The original title of ... *but the clouds* ... was 'Poetry only Love'.[66] Indeed, Laws argues that in using Beethoven's music in *Ghost Trio*, 'Beckett is exploring (and exploiting) the

---

[65] See Morton (2010) and Garrard (2012a) on Romantic constructions of nature. Scholarship has also examined Beckett's relation to the pastoral tradition, for example Hamilton (2002).

[66] UoR MS 1553/2.

very possibility of consolation and even transcendence through music, epitomised by the romantic idea of Beethoven' (2013, 156). The invocation of the
Romantic, expressive power of the music is therefore both exploited and
exposed:

> Beckett specifically draws on the spirit of German Romanticism that infuses
> the music, but does so precisely to deconstruct these ideas and put into
> question the possibility of simple solace or absolute redemption. The con-
> solation offered by the music is evoked but only insubstantially, as part of the
> play's examination of its own imagining and construction. (Laws, 2013, 133)

That framing of its own construction from fragments of previous iterations
relates to the visual as well as musical elements of the teleplay's composition.
Indeed, as Bignell argues, to engage with *Ghost Trio* as a viewer-listener is to
experience the defamiliarisation of the habitual conventions of watching television since it, along with other Beckett teleplays, 'challenge[s] the audience to
decode the play's dramatic form' (2009, 196). None of Beckett's television
plays include synchronised speech – words and image are separated through
voice-over so that the viewer has to actively work out or puzzle about the
relation between the voice and the figure. If television is usually associated with
a contemporary window onto the world, Beckett certainly 'makes it old', as
Herren has suggested, both through using anachronistic techniques associated
with an earlier era of television, and through including references to works from
other artistic media and from many other historical eras. The references to dust
evoke the Bible with its warnings of human pride in the face of inevitable
mortality and a time frame in which all human activity and self-inspection will
have faded into ghostly shadows.

This extra-human time frame is taken up again in ... *but the clouds* ..., whose
title is from W. B. Yeats' poem 'The Tower'. .... *but the clouds* ... also features
a male subject alone in an interior space, begging for the face of a woman to appear.
However the audiovisual construction of any coherent space or time is again
disrupted and fractured through several non-synchronised layers. The structure is
highly patterned, with the figure of the subject represented on one hand as an
almost indistinguishable shadow crouched over an 'invisible table' (Beckett, 1986,
417) as the visible form of the interior thinking or remembering subject, and, on the
other, a manikin or puppet, representing his 'exterior' or self-consciously staged
self, entering from darkness into a circle of light, apparently from walking the back
roads of the exterior world in his outerwear, signified by hat and greatcoat. The
figure moves only in straight lines due east (from the back roads) or west (from
having divested himself of hat and coat) or north (into the sanctum), with the
camera position at south: an entire world mapped within this small interior. On one

hand, the repeated attempts of M to stage and remember exactly his movements – 'Let us now make sure we have got it right' (419) – and his continual recourse to mathematics suggest an obsession with pattern and control, but, on the other, the satirical tone of his thoughts and his caricatured representations puncture and satirise these aspirations. However, unlike his puppet self who can be summoned and commanded at will, 'she' cannot be so commanded. M distinguishes three different forms of apparition: the woman's face appears and is gone, she appears and 'lingers', or she appears and mouths the last lines of W. B. Yeats' poem which evoke the impermanence of all human life and losses. Or, 'by far the commonest' she doesn't appear at all, and M has to resort to 'something else, more … rewarding, such as … such as … cube roots, for example' (421). As Anthony Paraskeva has argued, … *but the clouds* … stages 'the failure to find redemption in the muse-inspired imagination' (2017, 153).

… *but the clouds* … therefore critiques the desire for rational control imaged as a kind of director staging the audio and visual elements of the teleplay, and also introduces an alternative set of spatio-temporal frames associated with the feminine which escape the conscious imposition of form and pattern. It is the woman's face W which gives access to this vision of otherness. The feminine is associated here again with the Romantic muse, but, as in *Ghost Trio*, this female vision or visitation is presented not as a specific embodied female, but as a generic Romanticised image of 'spirit made light', the epitome of what the male subject is missing within those conventions. This is not a study of the material effects of gender on lived bodies, but a reflection on an inherited, gendered set of representations. On one hand, *Ghost Trio* and … *but the clouds* … privilege the male subject as the one who is actively longing and the female as the muse, but on the other, both these positions are seen as constructions generated from a set of historical texts and conventions: Beckett would not have been unaware that the letters M and W are inversions of each other. There is also a set of intermedial interchanges here, as the literary medium of poetry is translated into the face of a ghostly woman. Enoch Brater discusses the relationship between text and vision in this drama: 'It is difficult to tell [. . .] if image imitates words, or words imitate image: which illustrates which?' (Brater, 1987, 102). W mouths at first inaudibly, voiced by M, and then finally audibly, the last lines from Yeats' poem, which evokes a temporal horizon in which human life fades away: no more than 'the clouds of the sky … when the horizon fades … or a bird's sleepy cry … among the deepening shades' (Beckett, 1986, 422). However ironically the carefully staged preparation for the summoning of W is presented – Enoch Brater notes that Yeats' play *Words Upon the Window Pane* with its séance setting is also an intertext – the focus on the close-up of the woman's face and the final words of the poem retain the echoes of affective longing for comfort or company.

While both *Ghost Trio* and *... but the clouds ...* evoke layers of historical texts and images, the extra-temporal time frame of the divine re-emerges in *Nacht und Träume*. *Nacht und Träume* picks up the split screen of *... but the clouds ...* as representing both the figure in an interior scene and the interior mind or dreamscape of that figure. There is no spoken text but, as in *Ghost Trio*, music is used to create mood and narrative, here Schubert's eponymous lied. The figure of Dreamer A is shown falling asleep at his table, with little else to indicate period, while a separate screen shows the dreamt self of the dreamer B visited by a comforter, imaged solely by hands (which Beckett wanted to remain androgynous) and represented by the eucharistic objects of goblet and cloth.[67] The dream frame then fades, leaving A bereft. The teleplay is unusually devoid of Beckett's habitual satiric tone, but the overall impact is one of abandonment and the illusion of comfort, whether in divine grace or in the affective power of music and the arts. Laws argues that in *Nacht und Träume*:

> Beckett draws on the Romantic sensibility of the music, threading it into the
> fabric of the work, using its expressive power but also showing us how it is
> used. As in *Ghost Trio* (though with a different context and to different ends)
> he reflects back the ways in which we use music for sentimental succour, to
> call up and recall the affective qualities of particular ideas or memories, and
> even invites us back into that experience as we hear the music again. In this
> respect the play is both sentimental and not; the sentiment is simultaneously
> directly invoked and offered up as an object for reflection. (2013, 200)

These teleplays therefore acknowledge not just the human longing for another to fulfil the lacking self, but also the need to articulate, represent and reflect on that longing through human creative labour which is fuelled by its own history and traditions. And yet the teleplays also defamiliarise and decentre both the subjective longing and its representations especially in the Romantic tradition, by the focus on structure, system, technology and anachronistic televisual techniques, conventions, set and costume. The teleplays therefore seem to look back on humans and their histories as exhausted ghosts viewed from some time in a far future when all human traces may in fact have faded. The full force of Beckett's satiric critique of anthropocentric 'man' emerges in his final play composed for television.

Quad and *What Where*: Endgames of the Anthropocene

Quad and *What Where* continue a preoccupation with an extended spatio-temporal frame within which the human figures are depicted, but these teleplays move away from any focus on individual affective, imaginative or thought

---

[67] See Herren (2007, 155–6).

processes. Rather, *Quad* shows four figures differentiated only by the colour of
their gowns – red, yellow, blue or white – on a playing arena apparently
suspended in space scuttling towards a central point to the accompaniment of
percussive instruments, only to avoid that central point or 'danger zone'
(Beckett, 1986, 453) and return to the dark edges of the playing space. There
is no glimpse of interiority through spoken text or human sounds of any kind,
the figures are simply players and human activity is reduced or distilled to
repeated serial patterns with no end in sight. Indeed, *Quad II*, included when
Beckett saw the rushes of the play being replayed in black and white and
exclaimed that it could be 10,000 years later (Knowlson, 1996, 674), returns
to the tendency to place individual life in a much vaster spatio-temporal frame
where human intentionality and history fade into insignificance. Nevertheless,
Mary Bryden comments on 'the symptoms of trauma which gradually emerge
from the prolongation of the play [. . .] It is the existence of this nameless fear
which recruits *Quad* into the human domain and divorces it from the mechan-
ization of the dodged track' (1994, 111). As in the prose closed space texts,
although anthropocentric attempts to define, know and master human and other
life forms are framed and scrutinised, there are glimpses of an affective
compassion or tenderness for the subjected. Even that, though, can barely be
distinguished in Beckett's last work for television.

What Where is Beckett's last play for the theatre, written and produced in
1983, and his last directing work when he adapted it for SDR television in 1985
(Fehsenfeld, 1986). Although *What Where* was not originally written for the
small screen, the televisual version is such a radical critique of the anthropocentric drive for knowledge and control that it merits a concluding discussion in
this section. In the stage version, there are four players *'as alike as possible'*
(Beckett, 1986, 469), all with the *'same long grey gown'* and *'long grey hair'*
familiar from most of the male figures of Beckett's late drama for stage and
television, and indeed anticipated in the grey trailing gowns of 'Espace souterrain'. The names of the players are differentiated only by their vowels, BAM,
BEM, BIM and BOM. These named bodies do not speak, and the only voice is
that of BAM, listed separately as VOICE OF BAM (V) (469). The sameness
erodes any sense of individuality, and the voice of BAM is represented by
a megaphone, suggesting a medium of transmission and also foregrounding its
wish to dominate, to be heard above others. The drama consists of cycles of
interrogation of each player in order to uncover 'what' and 'where', accompanied by the threat to 'give him the works', as many scholars have noted,
associating processes of torture with 'a function of memory, remorse, and the
relentless need to tell a story' (Brater, 1987, 162). But these cycles of interrogation produce no knowledge or narrative, only the repetition of exits and

entrances with bowed or raised heads, while the voice of BAM notes the seasons passing. In an ironic citation of Schubert's Romantic song cycle *Die Winterreise* (*Winter Journey*), 'nature' here exists only as the repetition of cyclical time without progress:

> It is winter
> Without journey.
> Time passes.
> That is all.
> (Beckett, 1986, 476)

When Beckett revised the work for television, he worked closely with the technical team at SDR, especially Jim Lewis, a cameraman who Beckett particularly respected (Lewis, 1986). The stage drama became distilled even further and its time frame extended beyond that of mortal flesh, since the figures become represented only by faces like death masks and the action is reduced to these isolated faces fading in and out of visibility. Human existence is glimpsed as a flicker in the aeons of time, but what remains to echo throughout these sterile seasons is the anthropocentric drive to know and control which reduces the whole world, human and more than human, to cycles of coercion, leaving the questions of 'what' and 'where' unknown and unknowable. The only ending is when BAM terminates the 'session':

> Make sense who may.
> I switch off.
> (Beckett, 1986, 476)

Beckett's use of the television medium enabled him to explore a visually mediated environment where the camera could be used, as Crary has argued, to fracture any stable subject-object relation and to emphasise the ways in which the Anthropocene age has integrated technology into its modes of perception, control and concepts of subjectivity and embodiment. Ironically, this also contests the position of the human controller who is as much controlled by the technology as the inverse. The modes of perception that Beckett's teleplays set up actively involve the viewer in these technologised circuits where our control over the apparatus is challenged. As Pattie has commented, all of the mechanisms and circuits of these technologised environments or ecosystems exhaust themselves in their operation, confronting human observers also with the concept of their finitude not only individually, but also as a species. What remains is the persistent longing and drive to reflect back on histories of the 'human', however contested and unequal that category might be. Beckett's creative work repositions human agency in a non-anthropocentric time frame and a technologised, mediated environment in which the human as a species, its

texts and histories appear as ghosts and echoes, as at the end of the Yeats poem –
'like a bird's sleepy cry . . . among the deepening shades'.

5 Conclusion: Other Ways of Being

This study has drawn on the concept of ecosystems in order to investigate a selection of Beckett's works across different media where the focus is less on investigating a marginalised or fractured subjectivity than on the imaginative creation of worlds where the human species does not occupy a privileged place in the order of creation: rather, Beckett's human figures are trapped in a regulated system in which they have little agency. In much of his later work, the will to create, envisaged as an eye of prey, subjects human bodies to instrumental and objectifying observation and measurement, with apparent anthropological detachment. A creative impulse remains in the making or unmaking of these worlds which operates on the reader or spectator's perceptual, sensory and conceptual responses. Beckett draws on each medium to implicate the reader or the viewer in the controlling mechanisms of the work: *Catastrophe* is of course a metatheatrical example of this, where the Protagonist, who is being exploited as a spectacle in the service of the Director and his regime, is offered also to the gaze of the audience members who are then invited to reflect on their role as voyeurs. The stage itself becomes a space of ritual subjection of the Protagonist. In the diverse works discussed here, medium-specific technologies, in some cases translated into intermedial or transmedial modes of imagination, are crucial to Beckett's making of these apparently closed worlds and to the viewer's perception of them, including a self-conscious reflection on the exercise and visual consumption of surveillance and subjection. Yet Beckett's texts also invoke the vulnerability of human creatures to such modes of mechanised or technologised regulation and surveillance, which seems very contemporary and which accounts for the affective and poetic charge of his work.

Such a perspective also reflects on questions of agency and ethics that have been much debated in Beckett scholarship. Amanda Dennis has argued that 'Beckett's work may sketch plans for a more ecological, post-human version of agency, a more collaborative mode of "acting" that eases the divide between the human, the world of inanimate objects, and the earth' (Dennis, 2018, 8). *Quad*, for example, offers an alternative mode of agency less founded on individual will, suggesting that 'the players are part of a larger system – and, as such, driven by forces other than their own volition to move' (10). From an ecocritical perspective, Beckett's work is indeed highly critical or sceptical of human agency over others, the environment or even the self, portraying with forensic detail that agency and its technological extensions as objectifying and controlling. On one hand, such a scepticism about agency risks portraying humans as impotent to act in order to create less exploitative political, economic, social or environmental structures, but on the other, perhaps this is the beginning of an alternative foundation of our relationship to our planet and to our human and more than human cohabitants, based on 'kinship in mutual vulnerability' (Garrard, 2012b, 394).

A great deal of scope remains to investigate other texts or approaches to Beckett's work from an ecological perspective, including analyses of specific productions. The Paul Chan / Creative Time *Waiting for Godot* set in the flooded districts of New Orleans after Hurricane Katrina (2007) was interpreted as waiting for FEMA, the US federal emergency assistance agency, and emphasised that the impact of 'natural' emergencies is inseparable from political priorities (Chan, 2010). Ecological interpretations of the scenography of *Happy Days* include a landscape covered with plastic in a production at the Comédie de Béthune in France in 2010, a depopulated landscape glimpsed through a flooded contemporary kitchen in Katie Mitchell's 2015 production in Germany, or the 2018 production at the Manchester Royal Exchange, starring Maxine Peake, which featured an in-the-round island designed by Naomi Dawson whose bottom edges were scattered with discarded litter and debris.[68] The radical sense of dislocation and unhomeliness that Beckett's theatre opens up is likely to lead to new practical and theoretical interpretations as Beckett's work is increasingly invoked in relation to a growing realisation that we need new paradigms and practices that reposition the human in relation to the earth and its resources. Morton argues that art and aesthetics are central to the reimagining of 'how humans experience their place in the world' (2007, 2), and even concepts of human identity in relation to the shared environment: 'The point is to go against the grain of dominant, normative ideas about nature, but to do so in the name of sentient beings suffering under catastrophic environmental conditions' (12).

Beckett's work therefore resonates with Morton's concept of dark ecology, where the reorientation of the human in the face of impending catastrophe and possible demise inevitably prompts an affective response, whose articulation in art and culture may help us to respond to an unknown future and to a shared vulnerability to a biosphere that has been and continues to be damaged by human exploitation (Morton, 2007, 2016). Writing this Element during the coronavirus pandemic of 2020, when Beckett was a pervasive reference on

---

[68] For more information on Blandine Savetier's production of *Oh les beaux jours* at the Comédie de Béthune with Natalie Royer and Yann Collette, see Kelleher (2015); on Katie Mitchell's *Glückliche Tage* with Julie Wieninger as Winnie and Paul Herwig as Willie at the Deutsches Schauspielhaus, Hamburg, see McMullan (2018).

social media, reminded me of how often Beckett is invoked at moments of individual and communal crisis, from contemplating the end of life (see Barry, 2016), to thinking through issues of bearing witness to human perpetrated atrocities (Jones, 2011), to the very survival of our own and other species in an increasingly threatened biosphere.[69] The turn to Beckett, whose texts are saturated with layers of other philosophical, scientific, literary and artistic works, is also an encounter through a strange, expanded temporal lens with the fragments and traces of those histories of human thought and imagining, and indeed with the generations of scholars who have excavated and interpreted Beckett's texts and their contexts and genealogies. Beckett remains as productive, now as ever, in the attempts to rethink the human and to try to find other ways of being on this earth.

---

[69] See, for example, theatre critic Charles McNulty's argument that the COVID-19 pandemic revealed Beckett to be the ultimate realist: www.latimes.com/entertainment-arts/story/2020–05-25/coronavirus-pandemic-samuel-beckett [accessed 11 September 2020].

Bibliography

Abbott, H. Porter (2002), 'Beckett's Lost Worlds: The Artful Exhaustion of a 19th-Century Genre', *Journal of Beckett Studies*, 11:1, pp. 1–14.

Abram, David (1996), *The Spell of the Sensuous: Perception and Language in a More-than-Human World*, New York: Pantheon Books.

Ackerley, Chris (2005), 'Inorganic Form: Samuel Beckett's Nature', *Journal of the Australasian Universities Language and Literature Association*, 104, pp. 70–89.

Anderton, Joseph (2016), *Beckett's Creatures: Art of Failure after the Holocaust*, London: Bloomsbury Methuen Drama.

Arons, Wendy and Theresa J. May, eds (2012), *Readings in Performance and Ecology*, Basingstoke: Palgrave Macmillan.

Augustine of Hippo [*c*.390] (2004), *Expositions of the Psalms 121–150*, trans. Maria Boulding, New York: New City Press.

Balme, Christopher (2004), 'Rethinking the Relationship between Theatre and Media', in Christopher Balme and Markus Moninger (eds), *Crossing Media: Theater – Film – Fotografie – Neue Medien*, Munich: ePodium. https://epub.ub.uni-muenchen.de/13098/1/Balme_13098.pdf [accessed 14 April 2020].

Barry, Elizabeth (2016), 'Samuel Beckett and the Contingency of Old Age', *Samuel Beckett Today / Aujourd'hui*, 28:2, pp. 205–17.

Beckett, Samuel (1964), *How It Is*, London: John Calder.

Beckett, Samuel [1938] (1973), *Murphy*, London: Pan Books in association with Calder and Boyers.

Beckett, Samuel (1976), *The Beckett Trilogy: Molloy, Malone Dies, The Unnamable*, London: Picador.

Beckett, Samuel (1983), *Disjecta: Miscellaneous Writings and a Dramatic Fragment*, ed. Ruby Cohn, London: John Calder.

Beckett, Samuel (1986), *The Complete Dramatic Works*, London: Faber and Faber.

Beckett, Samuel (1995), *The Complete Short Prose 1929–1989*, ed. S. E. Gontarski, New York: Grove Press.

Beckett, Samuel (1996), *Eleutheria*, trans. Barbara Wright, London: Faber and Faber.

Beckett, Samuel (1999), *Beckett's Dream Notebook*, ed. John Pilling, Reading: Beckett International Foundation.

Beckett, Samuel (2014), *The Letters of Samuel Beckett, Vol. III: 1957–1965*, ed. George Craig, Martha Dow Fehsenfeld, Dan Gunn and Lois More Overbeck, Cambridge: Cambridge University Press.

Bignell, Jonathan (2009), *Beckett on Screen: The Television Plays*, Manchester: Manchester University Press.

Blackman, Jackie (2009), 'Post-war Beckett: Resistance, Commitment or Communist Krap?', in Russell Smith (ed.), *Beckett and Ethics*, London: Continuum, pp. 68–85.

Boxall, Peter (1998), 'Freedom and Cultural Location in *Eleutheria*', *Samuel Beckett Today / Aujourd'hui*, 7, pp. 245–59.

Brater, Enoch (1974), 'The Empty Can: Samuel Beckett and Andy Warhol', *Journal of Modern Literature*, 3:5, pp. 1255–64.

Brater, Enoch (1987), *Beyond Minimalism: Beckett's Late Style in the Theater*, Oxford: Oxford University Press.

Brater, Enoch (2011), *Ten Ways of Thinking about Beckett: The Falsetto of Reason*, London: Methuen Drama.

Bryden, Mary (1994), '*Quad*: Dancing Genders', *Samuel Beckett Today / Aujourd'hui*, 4, pp. 109–22.

Bryden, Mary, ed. (2013), *Beckett and Animals*, Cambridge: Cambridge University Press.

Carson, Rachel (1962), *Silent Spring*, Boston: Houghton Mifflin.

Caselli, Daniela (2005), *Beckett's Dantes: Intertextuality in the Fiction and Criticism*, Manchester: Manchester University Press.

Chan, Paul (2010), Waiting for Godot *in New Orleans: A Field Guide*, New York: Creative Time.

Chapple, Freda and Chiel Kattenbelt, eds (2006), *Intermediality in Theatre and Performance*, Amsterdam: Rodopi.

Cohn, Ruby (1967), '"Theatrum Mundi" and Contemporary Theatre', *Comparative Drama*, 1:1, pp. 28–35.

Cohn, Ruby (1980), *Just Play: Beckett's Theater*, Princeton, NJ: Princeton University Press.

Cohn, Ruby (2001), *A Beckett Canon*, Ann Arbor: University of Michigan Press.

Coleridge, Samuel Taylor [1817] (2014), *Biographia Literaria*, ed. Adam Roberts, Edinburgh: Edinburgh University Press.

Connor, Steven (1992), 'Between Theatre and Theory: "Long Observation of the Ray"', in John Pilling and Mary Bryden (eds), *The Ideal Core of the Onion: Reading Beckett Archives*, Reading: Beckett International Foundation, pp. 79–98.

Connor, Steven (2003), 'Beckett's Atmospheres', a paper given at the 'After Beckett / Après Beckett' conference in Sydney (January). http://stevenconnor .com/atmospheres-2.html [accessed 11 March 2018].

Connor, Steven (2006), 'Beckett and the World', Global Beckett Conference, University of Southern Denmark, Odense (26 October). http://stevenconnor .com/beckettworld.html [accessed 31 March 2020].

Connor, Steven (2014), *Beckett, Modernism and the Material Imagination*, Cambridge: Cambridge University Press.

Cordingley, Anthony (2018), *Samuel Beckett's How It Is: Philosophy in Translation*, Edinburgh: Edinburgh University Press.

Crary, Jonathan (1990), *Techniques of the Observer: On Vision and Modernity in the Nineteenth Century*, Cambridge MA: MIT Press.

Crutzen, Paul J. (2002), 'Geology of Mankind', *Nature*, 415:23. www .nature.com/articles/415023a [accessed 23 April 2020].

Curtius, Ernst Robert (1953), *European Literature and the Latin Middle Ages*, trans Willard R. Trask, Princeton, NJ: Princeton University Press.

Dante, Alighieri [1302–29] (2011), *The Divine Comedy, Volume III: Paradiso*, trans. Robert M. Durling, Oxford: Oxford University Press.

Davies, Paul (2006), 'Strange Weather: Beckett from the Perspective of Ecocriticism', in Stanley E. Gontarski and Anthony Uhlmann (eds), *Beckett after Beckett*, Gainesville: University of Florida Press, pp. 66–78.

Davis, Heather and Zoe Todd (2017), 'On the Importance of a Date, Or, Decolonizing the Anthropocene', *ACME: An International Journal for Critical Geographies*, 16:4, pp. 761–80.

Davis, Heather and Etienne Turpin, eds (2015), *Art in the Anthropocene: Encounters among Aesthetics, Politics, Environments and Epistemologies*, London: Open Humanities Press.

Dennis, Amanda (2018), 'Compulsive Bodies, Creative Bodies: Beckett and Agency in the 21st Century', *Journal of Beckett Studies*, 27:1, pp. 5–21.

Dennis, Amanda (2020), 'Introduction: Samuel Beckett and the Nonhuman', in Amanda Dennis, Thomas Thoelen, Douglas Atkinson and Sjef Houppermans (eds), *Samuel Beckett Today / Aujourd'hui*, 30:2. Special Issue: Samuel Beckett and the Nonhuman, pp. 151–60.

Descartes, René [1637] (2006), *A Discourse on the Method of Correctly Conducting One's Reason and Seeking Truth in the Sciences*, trans. Ian MacLean, Oxford: Oxford University Press.

Doane, Mary Ann (2003), 'The Close-Up: Scale and Detail in the Cinema', *differences: A Journal of Feminist Cultural Studies*, 14:3, pp. 89–111.

Dowd, Garin (2007), *Abstract Machines: Samuel Beckett and Philosophy after Deleuze and Guattari*, Amsterdam: Rodopi.

Fay, Jennifer (2018), *Inhospitable World: Cinema in the Time of the Anthropocene*, Oxford: Oxford University Press.

Fehsenfeld, Martha (1986), '"Everything Out but the Faces": Beckett's Reshaping of *What Where* for Television', *Modern Drama*, 29:2, pp. 229–40.

Foster, David (2012), 'Spatial Aesthetics in the Film Adaptation of Samuel Beckett's *Comédie*', *Screen*, 53:2, pp. 105–17.

Fraser, Graham (1995), 'The Pornographic Imagination in "All Strange Away"', *Modern Fiction Studies*, 41:3, pp. 515–30.

Fraser, Graham (2009), 'The Calligraphy of Desire: Barthes, Sade, and Beckett's *How It Is*', *Twentieth Century Literature*, 55:1, pp. 58–79.

Frost, Everett (1997) 'A "Fresh Go" for the Skull: Directing *All That Fall*, Samuel Beckett's Play for Radio', in Lois Oppenheim (ed.), *Beckett Directing Beckett*, Ann Arbor: University of Michigan Press, pp. 186–219.

Garrard, Greg (2012a), *Ecocriticism*, London: Routledge.

Garrard, Greg (2012b), '*Endgame*: Beckett's Ecological Thought', *Samuel Beckett Today / Aujourd'hui*, 23, pp. 383–97.

Germoni, Karine (2007) 'The Theatre of *Le Dépeupleur*', *Samuel Beckett Today / Aujourd'hui*, 18, pp. 297–311.

Gontarski, S. E. (1985), *The Intent of Undoing in Samuel Beckett's Dramatic Texts*, Bloomington: Indiana University Press.

Gontarski, S. E., ed. (1992), *The Theatrical Notebooks of Samuel Beckett: Endgame*, London: Faber and Faber.

Gontarski, S. E. (2017), *Beckett Matters: Essays on Beckett's Late Modernism*, Edinburgh: Edinburgh University Press.

Guattari, Felix (2000), *The Three Ecologies*, trans. Ian Pindar and Paul Sutton, London: Continuum.

Hamilton, Geoff (2002), 'Life Goes On: *Endgame* As Anti-Pastoral Elegy', *Modern Drama*, 45:4, pp. 611–27.

Haraway, Donna (2015), 'Donna Haraway in Conversation with Martha Kenney', in Heather Davis and Etienne Turpin (eds), *Art in the Anthropocene: Encounters among Aesthetics, Politics, Environments and Epistemologies*, London: Open Humanities Press, pp. 255–70.

Harries, Martin (2014), 'The End of a Trope for the World', in Björn Quiring (ed.), *If Then the World a Theatre Present: Revisions of the Theatrum Mundi Metaphor in Early Modern England*, Berlin: de Gruyter, pp. 221–39.

Harvey, Lawrence (1970), *Samuel Beckett: Poet and Critic*, Princeton, NJ: Princeton University Press.

Haverkamp, Anselm (2014), 'A Narrow Thing within One Word: The Foreclosure of Nature in Post-Shakespearean Worlds', in Björn Quiring (ed.), *If Then the World a Theatre Present: Revisions of the Theatrum Mundi Metaphor in Early Modern England*, Berlin: de Gruyter, pp. 133–51.

Heidegger, Martin (1977), *The Question Concerning Technology and Other Essays*, trans. W. Lovitt, New York: Harper and Row.

Herren, Graley (2007), *Samuel Beckett's Plays on Film and Television*, New York: Palgrave Macmillan.

Herren, Graley (2009), 'Different Music: Karmitz and Beckett's Film Adaptation of Comédie', *Journal of Beckett Studies*, 18:1–2, pp. 10–31.

Jones, David Houston (2008), '"So Fluctuant a Death": Entropy and Survival in *The Lost Ones* and *Long Observation of the Ray*', in Russell Smith (ed.), *Beckett and Ethics*, London: Continuum, pp. 118–33.

Jones, David Houston (2011), *Samuel Beckett and Testimony*, Basingstoke: Palgrave.

Judovitz, Dalia (2001), *The Culture of the Body: Genealogies of Modernity*, Ann Arbor: Michigan University Press.

Katz, Daniel (2009), 'What Remains of Beckett: Evasion and History', in Ulrika Maude and Mathew Feldman (eds), *Beckett and Phenomenology*, London: Continuum, pp. 144–57.

Kelleher, Joe (2015), 'Recycling Beckett', in Clair Finburgh and Carl Lavery (eds), *Rethinking the Theatre of the Absurd: Ecology, the Environment and the Greening of the Modern Stage*, London: Bloomsbury, pp. 127–46.

Kershaw, Baz (2007), *Theatre Ecology: Environments and Performance Events*, Cambridge: Cambridge University Press.

Kiryushina, Galina, Einat Adar and Mark Nixon, eds (2021), *Beckett and Technology*, Edinburgh: Edinburgh University Press.

Knowlson, James (1986), '*Ghost Trio / Geister Trio*', in Enoch Brater (ed.), *Beckett at 80 / Beckett in Context*, Oxford: Oxford University Press, pp. 193–207.

Knowlson, James (1996), *Damned to Fame: The Life of Samuel Beckett*, London: Bloomsbury.

Knowlson, James and John Haynes (2003), *Images of Beckett*, Cambridge: Cambridge University Press.

Knowlson, James and Dougald McMillan, eds (1993), *The Theatrical Notebooks of Samuel Beckett:* Waiting for Godot, London: Faber and Faber.

Knowlson, James and John Pilling (1979), *Frescoes of the Skull: The Later Prose and Drama of Samuel Beckett*, London: Calder.

Köhler, Wolfgang [1917] (1927), *The Mentality of Apes*, trans. Ella Winter, London: Routledge and Kegan Paul.

Kuhn, Annette (1985), *The Power of the Image: Essays on Representation and Sexuality*, London: Routledge and Kegan Paul.

Kurman, George (1975), 'Entropy and the "Death" of Tragedy: Notes for a Theory of Drama', *Comparative Drama*, 9:4, pp. 282–304.

Lamartine, Alphonse de (2005), *Méditations poétiques*, Chalon-sur-Seône: Éditions Ligaran.

Lavery, Carl (2018a), 'Ecology in Beckett's Theatre Garden: Ways to Cultivate the *Oikos*', *Contemporary Theatre Review*, 28:1, pp. 10–26.

Lavery, Carl, ed. (2018b), *Performance and Ecology: What Can Theatre Do?* London: Routledge.

Lavery, Carl and Clare Finburgh, eds (2015), *Rethinking the Theatre of the Absurd: Ecology, the Environment and the Greening of the Modern Stage*, London: Bloomsbury Methuen Drama.

Laws, Catherine (2013), *Headaches among the Overtones: Music in Beckett / Beckett in Music*, Amsterdam: Rodopi.

Laws, Catherine (2017), 'Imagining Radio Sound: Interference and Collaboration in the BBC Radio Production of Beckett's *All That Fall*', in David Addyman, Matthew Feldman and Erik Tonning (eds), *Samuel Beckett and BBC Radio: A Reassessment*, Basingstoke: Palgrave Macmillan, pp. 103–38.

Levin, David Michael, ed. (1993), *Modernity and the Hegemony of Vision*, Berkeley: University of California Press.

Lewis, Jim (1986), 'Beckett et la caméra', *Revue d'Esthétique*, numéro spécial hors série, pp. 371–9.

Little, James (2020), *Samuel Beckett in Confinement: The Politics of Closed Space*, London: Bloomsbury.

Lyons, Charles (1964), 'Beckett's *Endgame*: An Anti-myth of Creation', *Modern Drama*, 7:2, pp. 204–9.

Lyotard, Jean-François (1993), 'Oikos', in *Political Writings*, trans. Bill Readings and Kevin Paul Geiman, London: University College London Press, pp. 96–107.

Maier, Michael (2001), '*Geistertrio*: Beethoven's Music in Samuel Beckett's Ghost Trio', *Samuel Beckett Today / Aujourd'hui*, 11, pp. 267–78.

Maier, Michael (2002), '*Geistertrio*: Beethoven's Music in Samuel Beckett's Ghost Trio (Part 2)', *Samuel Beckett Today / Aujourd'hui*, 12, pp. 313–20.

Marranca, Bonnie (1996), *Ecologies of Theatre: Essays at the Century Turning*, Baltimore, MD: Johns Hopkins University Press.

Maude, Ulrika (2013), 'Pavlov's Dog and Other Animals', in Mary Bryden (ed.), *Beckett and Animals*, Cambridge: Cambridge University Press, pp. 82–93.

McMillan, Dougald and Martha Fehsenfeld (1988), *Beckett in the Theatre*, London: Calder and Riverrun.

McMullan, Anna (2010), *Performing Embodiment in Samuel Beckett's Drama*, London: Routledge.

McMullan, Anna (2018), 'Interview with Katie Mitchell', *Contemporary Theatre Review*, special issue on Staging Beckett and Contemporary Theatre and Performance Cultures, 28:1, pp. 127–32.

McMullan, Anna (2021), 'Technology and the Voices of the More Than Human in Beckett's *All That Fall*', in Nicholas Johnson, Mariko Tanaka and Laurens de Vos (eds), *Beckett's Voices / Voicing Beckett*, Leiden: Brill.

McTighe, Trish (2013), *The Haptic Aesthetic in Samuel Beckett's Drama*, Basingstoke: Palgrave Macmillan.

McTighe, Trish, Emilie Morin and Mark Nixon, eds (2020), *Samuel Beckett Today / Aujourd'hui* 30:1. Special Issue: Beckett and Intermediality.

Milutis, Joe (1996), 'Radiophonic Ontologies and the Avant-Garde', *Tulane Drama Review*, 40:3, pp. 63–79.

Moody, Alys (2017), 'A Machine for Feeling: *Ping*'s Posthuman Affect', *Journal of Beckett Studies*, 26:1, pp. 87–102.

Morin, Emilie (2014), 'Beckett's Speaking Machines: Sound, Radiophonics and Acousmatics', *Modernism/modernity*, 21:1, pp. 1–24.

Morin, Emilie (2017), *Beckett's Political Imagination*, Cambridge: Cambridge University Press.

Morton, Timothy (2007), *Ecology without Nature: Rethinking Environmental Aesthetics*, Cambridge, MA: Harvard University Press.

Morton, Timothy (2010), *The Ecological Thought*, Cambridge, MA: Harvard University Press.

Morton, Timothy (2013), *Hyperobjects: Philosophy and Ecology after the End of the World*, Minneapolis: University of Minnesota Press.

Morton, Timothy (2014), 'How I Learned to Stop Worrying and Love the Term *Anthropocene*', *Cambridge Journal of Postcolonial Literary Enquiry*, 1:2, pp. 257–64.

Morton, Timothy (2016), *Dark Ecology*, New York: Columbia University Press.

Murphy, Paul (1982), 'The Nature of Allegory in "The Lost Ones", or The Quincunx Realistically Considered', *Journal of Beckett Studies*, 7, pp. 71–88.

Nixon, Mark (2009), 'Samuel Beckett's "Film-Vidéo-Cassette projet"', *Journal of Beckett Studies*, 18:1–2, pp. 32–43.

Nixon, Mark (2014), 'Beckett's Unpublished Canon', in S. E. Gontarski (ed.), *Samuel Beckett and the Arts*, Edinburgh: Edinburgh University Press, pp. 282–305.

O'Hara, Dan (2010), 'The Metronome of Consciousness', *Samuel Beckett Today / Aujourd'hui*, 22, pp. 435–47.

Paraskeva, Anthony (2017), *Beckett and Cinema*, London: Bloomsbury.

Pattie, David (2018), '"At Me Too Someone Is Looking": Coercive Systems in Beckett's Theatre', *Samuel Beckett Today / Aujourd'hui*, 30:2, pp. 227–38.

Pethö, Ágnes (2011), *Cinema and Intermediality: The Passion for the In-Between*, Newcastle upon Tyne: Cambridge Scholars Publishing.

Piette, Adam (2011), 'Beckett, Affect and the Face', *Textual Practice*, 25:2, pp. 281–95.

Pilling, John (2006), *A Samuel Beckett Chronology*, Basingstoke: Palgrave Macmillan.

Plato [348 BCE] (2012), *Laws*, trans. Benjamin Jowett, Luton: Andrews UK.

Praz, Mario [1930] (1954), *The Romantic Agony*, trans. Angus Davidson, Oxford: Oxford University Press.

Quiring, Björn, ed. (2014), *If Then the World a Theatre Present: Revisions of the Theatrum Mundi Metaphor in Early Modern England*, Berlin: de Gruyter.

Rabaté, Jean-Michel (2016), *Think, Pig! Beckett at the Limit of the Human*, New York: Fordham University Press.

Rabaté, Jean-Michel (2020), 'Beckett's Sade / Barthes' Zade', *Samuel Beckett Today / Aujourd'hui*, 32:2, pp. 272–88.

Rada, Michelle (2018), 'Boring Holes: The Crystalline Body of Beckett's *The Lost Ones*', *Journal of Beckett Studies*, 27:1, pp. 22–39.

Schaumann Caroline and Heather I. Sullivan, eds (2017), *German Ecocriticism in the Anthropocene*, Basingstoke: Palgrave Macmillan.

Schneider, Alan (1995), 'On Directing Beckett's *Film*', *Samuel Beckett Today / Aujourd'hui*, 4, pp. 29–40.

Shakespeare, William (1986), *William Shakespeare: The Complete Works*, ed. Stanley Wells and Gary Taylor, Oxford: Clarendon Press.

Siess, Jürgen (2003), 'The Actor's Body and Institutional Tensions: From Act Without Words I to Not I', *Assaph*, 17–18, pp. 297–307.

Stengers, Isabelle in conversation with Heather Davis and Etienne Turpin (2014), 'Matters of Cosmopolitics: On the Provocations of Gaïa', in Etienne Turpin (ed.), *Architecture in the Anthropocene: Encounters among Design, Deep Time, Science and Philosophy*, Ann Arbor, MI: Open Humanities Press, pp. 171–82.

Tajiri, Yoshiki (2013), 'Beckett Coetzee and Animals' in Mary Bryden (ed.), *Beckett and Animals*, Cambridge: Cambridge University Press, pp. 27–39.

Tansley, Arthur George (1935), 'The Use and Abuse of Vegetational Concepts and Terms', *Ecology*, 16:3, pp. 284–307.

Tillyard, Eustace Mandeville Wetenhall (1943), *The Elizabethan World Picture*, London: Chatto and Windus.

Tonning, Erik (2007), *Samuel Beckett's Abstract Drama: Works for Stage and Screen 1962–85*, Bern: Peter Lang.

Tucker, David (2015), '"Beckett's Guignol Worlds": Arnold Geulincx and Heinrich von Kleist', in Matthew Feldman and Karim Mamdani (eds), *Beckett / Philosophy*, Stuttgart: ibidem, pp. 235–60.

Van Hulle, Dirk and Mark Nixon (2007), *Samuel Beckett Today / Aujourd'hui*, 18, Special Issue: Beckett and Romanticism.

Van Hulle, Dirk and Shane Weller (2018), *The Making of Samuel Beckett's* Fin de partie / Endgame. The Beckett Digital Manuscript Project 07. London: Bloomsbury.

Verhulst, Pim (2015), 'Just Howls from Time to Time: Dating *Pochade radiophonique*', *Samuel Beckett Today / Aujourd'hui*, 27, pp. 147–62.

Wallace-Wells, David (2019), *The Uninhabitable Earth: A Story of the Future*, London: Allen Lane (Penguin Random House).

Weathers, Kathleen C., David L. Strayer and Gene E. Likens, eds (2013), *Fundamentals of Ecosystem Science*, San Diego, CA: Elsevier.

Weber-Caflisch, Antoinette (1994), *Chacun son dépeupleur: sur Samuel Beckett*, Paris: Éditions de Minuit.

Weller, Shane (2006), *Beckett, Literature and the Ethics of Alterity*, Basingstoke: Palgrave Macmillan.

Weller, Shane (2008), 'Not Rightly Human: Beckett and Animality', *Samuel Beckett Today / Aujourd'hui*, 19:1, pp. 211–21.

Weller, Shane (2009), 'An Anethics of Desire: Beckett, Racine, Sade', in Russell Smith (ed.), *Beckett and Ethics*, London: Continuum, pp. 102–17.

Weller, Shane (2013), 'Forms of Weakness: Animalisation in Kafka and Beckett', in Mary Bryden (ed.), *Beckett and Animals*, Cambridge: Cambridge University Press, pp. 13–26.

White, Harry (1998), '"Something Is Taking Its Course": Dramatic Exactitude and the Paradigm of Serialism in Samuel Beckett', in Mary Bryden (ed.), *Samuel Beckett and Music*, Oxford: Clarendon Press, pp. 159–71.

Williams, Raymond (1977), *Marxism and Literature*, Oxford: Oxford University Press.

Zalasiewicz, Jan, Colin N. Waters, Colin P. Summerhayes et al. (2017), 'The Working Group on the Anthropocene: Summary of Evidence and Interim Recommendations', *Anthropocene*, 19, pp. 55–60.

Zilliacus, Clas (1976), *Beckett and Broadcasting: A Study of the Works of Samuel Beckett for and in Radio and Television*, Abo: Abo Akademi.

Zinman, Toby (1995), '*Eh Joe* and the Peephole Aesthetic', *Samuel Beckett Today / Aujourd'hui*, 4, pp. 53–64.

Films

Film, film, by Samuel Beckett, directed by Alan Schneider. Evergreen, 1964.

NotFilm, kino-film, directed by Ross Lipmann. Milestone Films in collaboration with Corpus Fluxus, 2016.

Cambridge Elements $^{\equiv}$

Beckett Studies

Dirk Van Hulle

University of Oxford

Dirk Van Hulle is Professor of Bibliography and Modern Book History at the University of Oxford and director of the Centre for Manuscript Genetics at the University of Antwerp.

Mark Nixon

University of Reading

Mark Nixon is Associate Professor in Modern Literature at the University of Reading and the Co-Director of the Beckett International Foundation.

About the Series

This series presents cutting-edge research by distinguished and emerging scholars, providing space for the most relevant debates informing Beckett studies as well as neglected aspects of his work. In times of technological development, religious radicalism, unprecedented migration, gender fluidity, environmental and social crisis, Beckett's works find increased resonance. Elements in Beckett Studies is a key resource for readers interested in the current state of the field.

Cambridge Elements ☰

Beckett Studies

Elements in the Series

Printed in the United States
By Bookmasters